SMASH REVIEWS FOR TH

THE COCKTAIL HOUR:
"Humor seems as natural as breathing to A. R. Gurney. THE
COCKTAIL HOUR is a beauty. . . . Could well be the best
play he has done. . . . Dazzling lines, so sensitive and deeply
rooted in each character . . . as fast as light and much
funnier."—*The New Yorker*

"A. R. Gurney is as funny as ever—at the top of his form. He
has new and witty observations to make—the zingers fly . . .
martini-fueled drawing room banter."
—Frank Rich, *The New York Times*

THE PERFECT PARTY:
"A daring leap forward . . . Gurney's funniest and most
theatrical play yet . . . offering surprises and laughter in equal
measure."—Frank Rich, *The New York Times*

"Entrancing . . . dazzling, entertaining."
—Clive Barnes, *New York Post*

ANOTHER ANTIGONE:
"A play that deals directly and seriously, though never solemnly,
with anti-Semitism. A synopsis can only hint at the dramatic
strength and richness of this splendid play, which is as
humorous, by the way, as its predecessors."—*The New Yorker*

"A provocative and perceptive play that is both entertaining
and thoughtful."—Rex Reed

A. R. GURNEY is the author of many highly acclaimed plays,
including *The Dining Room, Scenes from American Life,* and *The
Middle Ages.* He is also the author of three novels and the recipient
of the Drama Desk Award of Merit from the American Academy
and Institute of Arts and Letters.

Plays by A. R. Gurney

THREE PEOPLE
TURN OF THE CENTURY
THE RAPE OF BUNNY STUNTZ
THE COMEBACK
THE PROBLEM
THE LOVE COURSE
THE OLD ONE-TWO
THE OPEN MEETING
THE GOLDEN FLEECE
THE DAVID SHOW
SCENES FROM AMERICAN LIFE
CHILDREN
RICHARD CORY
THE MIDDLE AGES
THE WAYSIDE MOTOR INN
THE GOLDEN AGE
THE DINING ROOM
WHAT I DID LAST SUMMER
SWEET SUE
ANOTHER ANTIGONE
THE PERFECT PARTY
THE COCKTAIL HOUR
LOVE LETTERS

Novels

THE GOSPEL ACCORDING TO JOE
ENTERTAINING STRANGERS
THE SNOW BALL

The Cocktail Hour
And Two Other Plays:
Another Antigone
and *The Perfect Party*

by A. R. Gurney
with an Introduction by the Playwright

A PLUME BOOK

PLUME
Published by the Penguin Group
Penguin Books USA Inc., 375 Hudson Street, New York, New York
10014, U.S.A.
Penguin Books Ltd, 27 Wrights Lane, London W8 5TZ, England
Penguin Books Australia Ltd, Ringwood, Victoria, Australia
Penguin Books Canada Ltd, 2801 John Street, Markham, Ontario, Canada
L3R 1B4
Penguin Books (N.Z.) Ltd, 182-190 Wairau Road, Auckland 10, New Zealand

Penguin Books Ltd, Registered Offices: Harmondsworth, Middlesex, England

Published by Plume, an imprint of New American Library, a division of Penguin
Books USA Inc.

SPECIAL NOTE ON MUSIC AND RECORDINGS

For performance of such music and recordings mentioned in this play as are in copyright, the permission of the copyright owners must be obtained; or other music and recordings in the public domain substituted.

 REGISTERED TRADEMARK—MARCA REGISTRADA

Library of Congress Cataloging-in-Publication Data

Gurney, A. R. (Arthur Ramsdell), 1930–
    The cocktail hour and two other plays : Another Antigone and
The perfect party / by A. R. Gurney ; with an introduction by the
playwright.
      p.   cm.
    ISBN 0-452-26338-7
    I. Gurney, A. R. (Arthur Ramsdell), 1930–   Cocktail hour. 1989.
II. Gurney, A. R. (Arthur Ramsdell), 1930–   Perfect party. 1989.
III. Gurney, A. R. (Arthur Ramsdell), 1930–   Another Antigone.
1989.   IV. Title.
PS3557.U82C6 1989
812'.54—dc20   89-8814
                                          CIP

First Plume Printing, November, 1989

2 3 4 5 6 7 8 9

PRINTED IN THE UNITED STATES OF AMERICA

Introduction

One of my favorite passages in Shakespeare occurs toward the end of *Antony and Cleopatra*, when the Egyptian queen, preparing for her death, pauses to imagine her story being staged in Rome:

> . . . the quick comedians
> Extemporally will stage us and present
> Our Alexandrian revels. Antony
> Shall be brought drunken forth, and I shall see
> Some squeaking Cleopatra boy my greatness
> I' th' posture of a whore. (V, ii, 219–223)

The audacity of this moment never ceases to amaze me. Shakespeare, at the climax of his play, about to swing into one of the most beautiful death scenes ever written, chooses suddenly to deplore the vulgarities of the very medium in which he has chosen to tell his story. He knew that the actor delivering these lines would himself be a "squeaking" boy, who might easily play Cleopatra with stock posturings, just as the actor playing Antony might well ham up the drunkenness. Indeed, at the very point in the play where you'd think Shakespeare would be doing his utmost to get us to suspend our disbelief and lose ourselves in the plight of his heroine, Shakespeare pulls us out of it, reminding us that we are seeing an actor playing a role on a stage, whose performance may even be a parody of what the author intended.

People in academia like to call this tendency of art to curl back on itself "self-reflexiveness," but whatever it is, it seems to endow us with a double perspective toward what we are looking at. In the case of Shakespeare's play, we find ourselves both caught up in Cleopatra's impending doom, and at the same time made aware of the limitations of the form in which she is being presented to us. Just as Antony and Cleopatra have been unable to confine themselves to the responsible roles which world politics had asked them to play, so is the stage an inadequate arena to express the transcendent feelings which have brought them down. Ultimately, I think we are reminded of the inability of art to capture life, of shape to master shapelessness, of Roman order to capture watery Egypt, even as we see Shakespeare attempt to do all these things through the vulgar medium of the theatre.

Descending now from the sublime to the prosaic, I want to suggest that I myself have tried to achieve something of this same sort of double vision in the three plays published here. *Another Antigone* is about, and should constantly remind us that it is about, both its similarity to and difference from its Greek counterpart. *The Perfect Party*, written as a kind of satyr play to follow it, tries to underscore the connections between a social gathering and the very theatrical event the audience is actually attending. Finally, *The Cocktail Hour*, which ostensibly would seem to be the most realistic of the three, is, in another sense, the most theatrically self-conscious, since it is most of all about itself, and continually calls attention to its own stagecraft.

Possibly what I think I am doing in my plays is something all playwrights do, all the time. After all, most plays are ultimately about role-playing and performance, leading to some sort of unmasking at the end, and it's hard to find any good play which doesn't, in one way or another, display its own theatricality. One might also argue that this self-reflexiveness is simply a characteristic of most twentieth-century art forms. Modern painting, one might say, is really about the nature of paint, and color, and the flatness of the canvas; modern fiction is more and more about writing and story-making; the best movies could be said to be about motion, the best poetry about the nature of poetry. It is

natural, then, that anyone who chooses to write a play—
that is, chooses to write something to be performed on a
stage by actors in front of an audience—would be obsessed
by the very characteristics of the medium he has chosen.

What has he chosen, in this case? A tight, restricted form
where everything unessential must be rigorously eliminated,
and where every line, presumably, must forward the action
toward a climax and conclusion; a collaborative form which
is to a large extent dependent on the director, the actors,
and the designers, all of whom must respond to the text
with some kind of common trust and sensibility; and finally
a precarious form which is beset today by stringent economic considerations, so that the size of its cast, its scenic
requirements, the number of costumes it needs are all
important factors in the decision of whether it will ever be
produced at all. And, of course, an unproduced play is
still-born. Therefore, if a writer is going to commit himself
to all these restrictions, it makes sense to embrace and
celebrate them, rather than disguise them or pretend they
aren't there. If he is unhappy with them, he will probably
be much more at home in the fluid and liberated worlds of
the movies or television.

So maybe this obsessional playfulness I find emerging in
these plays of mine comes with the territory. Maybe it also
comes from having been involved with the theater for a long
time. To call again on exalted examples, Shakespeare's
work seems to become particularly conscious of its theatrical underpinnings toward the end of his career. Ibsen's final
plays, too, seem to be very much aware of their own
limitations, as they groan and stretch to break the confines
of fourth-wall realism. I myself have been writing plays of
one kind or another for almost forty years, and more and
more I find myself prowling around this cell I have put
myself in, testing its possibilities, and at least pretending to
cherish its restrictions. If I got out, I think I'd be totally
paralyzed by the unfamiliar freedom.

Yet what a strange, peculiar cage it is, so steeped in
traditions, so beset with traps, so inimicable to the cinematic
jump-cutting and fast-forwarding of contemporary Ameri-

can life. Choosing to write a play today is like choosing to buy a viola di gamba. Obsolete though it may be, once you've brought it home, you might as well try to get it to make its own particular kind of music. It makes no sense to force it to behave like a Moog synthesizer.

I suppose it's a poor idea for a writer to attempt to analyze his own work. The critics are supposed to do that for us, and over the years, I guess they have, for better or worse. It's only because I see myself rounding the last bend of what has been a long road that I'm now tempted to glance over my shoulder and see where I've been and what I've been up to. In any case, I notice that I can't seem to write a play without both testing and celebrating the borders of the form. For example, in *The Dining Room*, I try to confine myself to a single room and six actors, while covering fifty years and presenting over fifty characters. In *Sweet Sue*, I try to expand the dimensions of a simple love affair by telling the same story from the different perspectives of two sets of actors, performing simultaneously. In *Another Antigone*, I try to work with and against the great Greek tragedy; in *The Perfect Party*, I try to do a series of stretch exercises with form and language; and in *The Cocktail Hour*, I try to punch through the shop-worn conventions of a domestic comedy of manners by sharing with the audience the very structure of the play as it is being performed.

Furthermore, it occurs to me that most of my plays seem to be *about* people trying to test, stretch, or break the social restrictions which hem them in. In *Children*, everyone in the family tries unsuccessfully to celebrate a sense of independence on the day before the fourth of July. In *Richard Cory*, the hero tries to break out of the tight obligations of the world he was born into, even as I, the playwright, push against the confines of the Robinson poem. In *The Middle Ages*, again, the hero is constantly escaping from the cage of his upbringing, and constantly returning to it. In *What I Did Last Summer*, I try to present a contemporary version of the old Colonial captivity story, where a boy is "captured" by an Indian, taught a new kind of freedom, but returned to the "stockade" at the end.

These characters struggling to break the bonds of the world they were born into, and these plays pressing against the limitations of their own form, give my work, I hope, a theatricality which undercuts the conventions of realistic drama and the complacencies of the upper-middle-class milieu which I tend to write about. On the other hand, these effects can lead to trouble. By constantly calling attention within my plays to the fact that they are plays, I've pretty much seen to it that they won't be movies or television shows. They are what they are, and they don't seem to want to be anything else. Another disadvantage would seem to be that this built-in "playfulness," along with the fact that I write about WASPS, seems to open me up to the charge of being shallow and superficial. I suppose it's natural that if I keep reminding an audience that it is in a theater watching a play, and if I keep giving them characters who, unlike most Americans, are locked into traditional roles, I run the risk of preventing people from penetrating this theatricality and identifying with the people on stage. In everything I write, I always persuade myself that I'm dealing with complex characters in a profound way, but sometimes I guess it looks as if I'm just kidding.

On the other hand, this theatricality I've been talking about has some advantages. In the course of trying to get at the theatrical essense of a piece, I've found myself eliminating minor characters, restricting the number of sets, and sometimes asking actors to play many different roles. The result is that I've written a number of plays which are at least easy to do, and hence accessible to a large number of theaters. Though New York seems to be the center of theater in America, I don't think it's the center of the universe, and once a play has run the gauntlet on Manhattan island, I'm delighted for it to go on and be performed elsewhere in the country and in the world. I also persuade myself that this presentational quality which informs my plays may lead, if it works right, and if all the other essential elements of a production are working right, to a wonderful pay-off: namely, this sense of a double vision, whereby you can both respond to the life presented on stage and at the same time be aware of this confining, precarious, exasperatingly marvelous medium which is attempting to reflect it.

THE
COCKTAIL HOUR

The Cocktail Hour had its world premiere at the Old Globe Theatre, San Diego, California, on June 2, 1988. It was produced in New York by Roger L. Stevens, Thomas Viertel, Steven Baruch and Richard Frankel at the Promenade Theatre, where it opened on October 20, 1988. In both instances, it was directed by Jack O'Brien, while the scenery and costumes were by Steven Rubin and the lighting by Kent Dorsey. The production stage manager was Douglas Pagliotti. The managing director of the Old Globe, Thomas Hall, was the associate producer on the New York production. The cast, in order of appearance, was as follows:

BRADLEY	Keene Curtis
JOHN	Bruce Davison
ANN	Nancy Marchand
NINA	Holland Taylor

CAST

BRADLEY
ANN   his wife
JOHN   their son
NINA   their daughter

The play takes place during early evening in early fall in the mid-seventies, in a city in upstate New York.

The set is basically realistic, but should also be vaguely theatrical, reminding us subliminally of those photographs of sets of American drawing room comedies in the thirties or forties, designed by Donald Oenslager or Oliver Smith. In any case, it is a lovely step-down living room, with an arched entrance leading to a front hall, and perhaps the start of a staircase. There is an antique writing desk, a working fireplace with a mantelpiece, a fire bench, and a pretty good Impressionist painting hanging over it. The Upstage wall is full of good books, all hard-back, some leatherbound sets, some large art books, all neatly organized. The room also contains a baby grand piano on which are a number of black-and-white family photographs framed in silver or leather: portraits of children, snapshots of children at sports, pictures of dogs, large group shots of families, an occasional faded photograph of a nineteenth-century couple. Downstage, of course, is a large comfortable couch with a coffee table in front of it, along with several other comfortable chairs and a movable footstool. There might be a corner china cabinet displaying excellent china. All the furniture looks old and waxed and clean. There's a thick, warm Persian rug on the floor. Through the windows, a few barren branches are seen in the early evening light. The overall effect should not be opulent or grandiose or particularly trendy, but rather tasteful, comfortable, and civilized, an oasis of traditional warmth and solid good taste, a haven in a heartless world. On the coffee table, noticeably set apart from the china ashtrays and other objects, is a thick manuscript in a black cover.

ACT I

AT RISE: *The stage is empty. The light from the windows indicates early evening, early fall. After a moment,* BRADLEY *enters, carrying a silver ice bucket. HE is in his seventies and very well dressed. HE is followed by his son* JOHN, *who is in his early forties and more informally dressed.* JOHN *carries a silver tray with several liquor bottles and glasses on it.*

BRADLEY: *(Turning on the light in the hall)* This is what's called bringing the mountain to Mohammed.

JOHN: Right.

BRADLEY: Otherwise we'd have to trek all the way back to the pantry whenever we needed to return to the well.

JOHN: Makes sense to me.

BRADLEY: *(Setting down the ice bucket on the table behind the couch)* Of course when we had maids, it was different. You could just push the buzzer, and say bring this, bring that, and they'd bring it.

JOHN: *(Setting down the tray)* I remember.

BRADLEY: Not that they could mix a drink. They couldn't make a martini to save their skin. But they could make ice, bring water, pass cheese. It was very pleasant.

JOHN: Before the war.

7

BRADLEY: That damn war. Those Germans have a lot to answer for. Well. Let's see . . . What are we missing? . . . Have we got the lemon for your mother's martini?

JOHN: *(Taking it out of his pocket)* It's right here, Pop.

BRADLEY: Your mother likes a small twist of lemon in her martini.

JOHN: I know.

BRADLEY: And my Cutty Sark scotch.

JOHN: Oh yes.

BRADLEY: *(Looking at the label)* It's a good scotch. Not a great scotch, but a good one. I always enjoy the picture on the label. The American clipper ships were the fastest in the world. Magnificent vessels. Beautifully built. Made our country great.

JOHN: The *Cutty Sark* was English, Pop.

BRADLEY: I know that. I'm speaking generally.

JOHN: Actually the clipper ships only lasted a few years.

BRADLEY: Not true.

JOHN: Only a few—before steam.

BRADLEY: Not true at all.

JOHN: I think so, Pop.

BRADLEY: I wish your brother were here. He'd know. He knows all there is to know about boats.

JOHN: *(Going to bookcase)* I'll look it up.

BRADLEY: Never mind. I said, *never mind.* We are not going to waste the evening in pedantic arguments.
(JOHN returns from the bookcase.)
Now look what I did. I brought out a whole bottle of soda water. Automatically. Thinking your brother *would* be here. Won't drink anything else. Never did.

JOHN: Smart man.

BRADLEY: I telephoned him yesterday. Tried to get him to come up. "Come on, Jigger," I said. "Join us. John's coming. Your sister will be here. We'll all have cocktails and your mother will provide an excellent dinner. You can play the piano. We'll all gather around the piano and sing. Bring Sylvia, if you want. Bring the children. I'll pay for the whole thing." But no. Wouldn't do it. Jigger's a very positive person, once he's made up his mind.

JOHN: It's a tough trip for him, Pop.

BRADLEY: I know that.

JOHN: He's working weekends now. They've put him back in sales.

BRADLEY: We all have to sell. One way or another.

JOHN: He's looking for another job.

BRADLEY: I know all that. You don't need to tell me that. I'm in touch with him all the time.
(HE *returns to the bar.*)
What'll you have, by the way?

JOHN: Some of that soda water, actually.

BRADLEY: You?

JOHN: That's what I'll have.

BRADLEY: You're the one who likes to tuck it away.

JOHN: Not tonight.

BRADLEY: And why not, may I ask?

JOHN: It makes me say and do things I'm sorry for later.

BRADLEY: That's the fun of it.

JOHN: Not for me.

BRADLEY: You're not in difficulty, are you?

JOHN: No.

BRADLEY: You're not in one of those organizations that make you give it up?

JOHN: I just like to keep a lid on myself, Pop.

BRADLEY: Suit yourself.
(Pours him a glass of soda water)
Soda water it is. What is it Lord Byron tells us? "Let us have wine and women, mirth and laughter; sermons and soda water the day after" . . . Maybe you'll change your mind later on.

JOHN: Maybe I will.

BRADLEY: *(Now pouring his own scotch and water very carefully)* Of course, nobody drinks much these days. At least not with any relish. Marv Watson down at the club is now completely on the wagon. You sit down beside him at the big table, and what's he drinking? Orange juice. I said, "Am I confused about the time, Marv? Are we having breakfast?" Of course the poor thing can't hear, so it doesn't make any difference. But you go to parties these days and even the young people aren't drinking. I saw young Kathy Bickford at the Shoemaker wedding. Standing on the sidelines, looking very morose indeed. I went up to her and said, "What's that strange concoction you've got in your hand, Kathy?" She said, "Lemon Squirt." I said, "What?" She said, "Sugar-free, noncarbonated Lemon Squirt." So I said, "Now, Kathy, you listen to me. You're young and attractive, and you should be drinking champagne. You should be downing a good glass of French champagne, one, two, three, and then you should be out there on that dance floor, kicking up your heels with every usher in sight. And after you've done that, you should come right back here, and dance with me!" Of course, she walked away.
(HE finishes making his drink.)
They all walk away these days. I suppose I'm becoming a tiresome old fool.

JOHN: Hardly, Pop.

BRADLEY: Yes, well, I can still keep the ball in the air, occasionally. I gave a toast at the Shoemakers' bridal dinner. It went over very well.

JOHN: Mother told me.

BRADLEY: Oh yes. I made a few amusing remarks. I complimented the bride. You know Sarah Shoemaker? She's terribly tall. She towers over the groom. So I began by saying she stoops to conquer.

JOHN: That's a good one, Pop.

BRADLEY: Yes, they liked that. I can still get on my feet if called upon. They still want me to be the Master of Ceremonies at the annual fund raiser for the art gallery. They still ask me to do that.

JOHN: That's great, Pop.

BRADLEY: Of course, we all know what Emerson says, "The music that can deepest reach, and cure all ills, is cordial speech." Doesn't Emerson tell us that?

JOHN: I think he does, Pop.

BRADLEY: You're the publisher in the family. You should know.

JOHN: *(Going to bookcase again)* Let me look it up.

BRADLEY: It doesn't matter.

JOHN: It'll be right here, in Bartlett's.
(Takes down a book)

BRADLEY: No! We are not going to destroy the rhythm of the conversation with a lot of disruptive excursions to the bookcase.

JOHN: *(Putting the book back)* O.K.

BRADLEY: Besides, I know Emerson said it. I'm positive.

JOHN: O.K., Pop.

(BRADLEY *sits in what is obviously his special chair.*)

BRADLEY: *(After a pause)* Well. Your mother tells me you've written a play.

JOHN: That's right.

BRADLEY: Another play.

JOHN: Right.

BRADLEY: *(Indicating manuscript on table)* Is that it?

JOHN: That's it.

BRADLEY: Do you think this one will get on?

JOHN: I think so.

BRADLEY: Some of them don't, you know.

JOHN: I know that, Pop.

BRADLEY: I don't mean just yours. Apparently it's a very difficult thing to get them done.

JOHN: That's for sure.

BRADLEY: Of course nobody goes to the theater any more. Ted Moffatt just made a trip to New York to see his new grandson. I said, "Did you go to the theater, Ted? Did you see any new plays?" He said he did not. He said all they do these days in the theatre is stand around and shout obscenities at each other. And then take off their clothes. Ted said he wouldn't be caught dead at the theater. And Ted was once a big theater-goer.

JOHN: There's some good stuff down there, Pop.

BRADLEY: For you, maybe. Not for me. *(Pause)* We liked that play of yours we saw in Boston.

JOHN: Thanks.

BRADLEY: Done at some college, wasn't it?

JOHN: Boston University.

BRADLEY: We liked that one. Your mother particularly liked it. She thought it was quite amusing.

JOHN: Tell the critics that.

BRADLEY: Oh well, the critics. They're not infallible.

JOHN: I'll keep that in mind, Pop.
(Pause)

BRADLEY: We liked that little play of yours we saw in New York a couple of years ago.

JOHN: I thought you *didn't* like it.

BRADLEY: No, we did. Miserable little theater. Impossible seats. Impossible bathrooms. But the play had charm.

JOHN: Thanks, Pop.

BRADLEY: Or at least the actress did. What was her name again?

JOHN: Swoosie Kurtz.

BRADLEY: Yes. Swoosie Kurtz. Amusing name. Amusing actress. I hear she's gone on to do very well. Your mother saw her on television.

JOHN: She's great.

BRADLEY: Lovely profile. Lovely shoulders. She was very attractive in your play.

JOHN: I'll tell her.

BRADLEY: Yes, do. Tell her your father liked her very much.
(Pause. HE *eyes the manuscript on the coffee table.)*
And now you've written another one.

JOHN: Tried to.

BRADLEY: Looks a little long.

JOHN: They'll make me cut it.

BRADLEY: I hope they make you cut it a good deal.

JOHN: They probably will.

BRADLEY: Nobody likes long plays.

JOHN: I know that, Pop.

BRADLEY: Everyone likes to get it over with promptly, and go home to bed.

JOHN: I know.

BRADLEY: Will Swoosie Kurtz be in this one?

JOHN: I doubt it.

BRADLEY: I hope you get someone who's just as much fun.

JOHN: This play's a little different, Pop.

BRADLEY: Different? How is it different?

JOHN: It's not as light as the others.

BRADLEY: Don't tell me you're getting gloomy in your middle years.

JOHN: Not gloomy exactly, Pop.

BRADLEY: Are people going to scream and shout in this one?

JOHN: They might raise their voices occasionally.

BRADLEY: Are they going to take off their clothes?

JOHN: No, they won't do that, I promise.

BRADLEY: Put Swoosie Kurtz in it. She wouldn't shout. Though I suppose I wouldn't mind if she took off her clothes.
(Pause)

JOHN: This one's about us, Pop.

BRADLEY: Us?

JOHN: The family.

BRADLEY: Oh really?

JOHN: This one cuts pretty close to home.
(Pause)

BRADLEY: Oh well. I understand that. You have to deal with what you know. I do it when I'm toastmaster. I sometimes mention your mother. I refer occasionally to you children. At the Shoemakers' wedding, I told an amusing story about Jigger.

JOHN: This one's about you, Pop.

BRADLEY: Me?

JOHN: You.

BRADLEY: Just me?

JOHN: No, no. Mother's in it, of course. And Nina. And Jigger's referred to a lot. And I put myself in it. But I think it centers around you.

BRADLEY: Me.

JOHN: I thought I better tell you that, Pop.

BRADLEY: And it's going on?

JOHN: It's supposed to.

BRADLEY: In New York?

JOHN: That's the talk.

BRADLEY: When?

JOHN: Soon. Supposedly.
(Pause)

BRADLEY: Do you use our names?

JOHN: Of course not, Pop.

BRADLEY: But it's recognizably us.

JOHN: By people who know us.

BRADLEY: What about people who don't know us?

JOHN: They'll sense it's a personal play.
(Pause)

BRADLEY: I suppose you make cracks.

JOHN: Cracks?

BRADLEY: Wisecracks. Smart remarks.

JOHN: Not really.

BRADLEY: "Not really." What does that mean, "not really"?

JOHN: I just try to show who we are, Pop.

BRADLEY: Oh, I'm sure. I know what you write. I remember that crack you made about your grandmother in one of your plays.

JOHN: What crack?

BRADLEY: You know very well what crack. You poked fun at her. You ridiculed her. My dear sweet mother who never hurt a fly. That gracious lady who took you to the Erlanger Theatre every Saturday afternoon. That saint of a woman without whom you wouldn't even know what a play *was*!

JOHN: I didn't ridicule her, Pop.

BRADLEY: People laughed. I was there. I heard them laugh at your grandmother. Complete strangers roaring their heads off at my poor dear mother—I can't discuss it.

JOHN: Come on, Pop.

BRADLEY: I don't think you've written anything in your life where you haven't sneaked in a lot of smart-guy wisecracks about our family and our way of life.

JOHN: Please, Pop . . .

BRADLEY: That story you wrote at boarding school, that show you did at college . . .

JOHN: You never came to that show.

BRADLEY: I didn't want to come. I knew, I *knew* what you'd say.

JOHN: It was just fun, Pop.

BRADLEY: Oh yes? Well, your idea of fun and my idea of fun are very different. My idea does not include making fools out of your family.

JOHN: Oh Jesus.

BRADLEY: And don't swear! It's demeaning to both of us.

JOHN: O.K., O.K. I'm sorry.
(Pause)

BRADLEY: And you've found producers for this thing?

JOHN: Yes.

BRADLEY: They'll lose their shirt.

JOHN: Maybe.

BRADLEY: They'll go completely bankrupt.

JOHN: Come on, Pop.

BRADLEY: What did that critic say about your last play? What was his remark?

JOHN: He said we weren't worth writing about.

BRADLEY: There you are. You see? Nobody cares about our way of life.

JOHN: I care, Pop.

BRADLEY: You? You've never cared in your life. You've gone out of your way *not* to care. Where were you for our fortieth anniversary? Where were you for my seventy-fifth birthday?

JOHN: You said not to come.

BRADLEY: I didn't want you snickering in the corner, making snide remarks. Oh God, I should have known. I should have known that's why you came up here this weekend. Not to visit your parents in their waning years. Not to touch base with the city that nourished you half your life. Oh no. Nothing like that. Simply to announce that you plan to humiliate us all in front of a lot of strangers in New York City.

JOHN: I came home to get your permission, Pop.

BRADLEY: My permission?

JOHN: I haven't signed any contract yet.

BRADLEY: Then don't.

JOHN: *(After a moment)* All right, I won't.

BRADLEY: How can I give you permission for a thing like that?

JOHN: All right, Pop.

BRADLEY: How can I approve of someone fouling his own nest?

JOHN: I don't foul—

BRADLEY: How can I possibly seal my own doom?

JOHN: Oh, come on, Pop.

BRADLEY: I suppose I have no legal recourse.

JOHN: The play's *off*, Pop.

BRADLEY: I mean, you don't need to write plays anyway. You have a perfectly good job in publishing.

JOHN: That just keeps me going, Pop.

BRADLEY: It's a fine job. It's a solid, dependable, respectable job.

JOHN: It's not what I really want to do.

BRADLEY: Well, do it anyway. Most men in this world spend a lifetime doing what they don't want to do. And they work harder at it than you do.

JOHN: Come on, Pop . . .

BRADLEY: After I'm dead, after your mother's dead, after everyone you can possibly hurt has long since gone, then you can write your plays. And you can put them on wherever you want—New York, Hollywood, right here in Memorial Auditorium, I don't care. But not now. Please.

JOHN: O.K.

BRADLEY: I'm tired.

JOHN: O.K., Pop.

BRADLEY: I'm not well.

JOHN: I know, Pop.

BRADLEY: I'm not well at all.

JOHN: Case closed, Pop. Really.

BRADLEY: Thank you very much.
(Pause. THEY *are awkward alone.)*
Sure you don't want a drink?

JOHN: No thanks.
(Pause)

BRADLEY: Where's your mother? . . . Suddenly I thoroughly miss your mother.
(Going to doorway, calling off)
Darling, where are you?

ANN'S VOICE: (Offstage) I'm bringing cheese!

BRADLEY: *(To* JOHN*)* She's bringing cheese. *(Eying manuscript)* Did you tell her about this play?

JOHN: Yes.

BRADLEY: Did she read it?

JOHN: She said she didn't want to.

BRADLEY: Why not?

JOHN: I'm not sure . . .

BRADLEY: That's the trouble. We never are, with your mother.

(ANN *enters, carrying a plate of crackers and cheese.* SHE *is a lovely woman, richly and fashionably dressed.*)

ANN: There.

(BOTH MEN immediately get to their feet.)
I think I may have established a modicum of order in the kitchen.

(SHE *waits for* JOHN *to move his script out of the way, then puts the plate of hors d'oeuvres on the coffee table.*)
And now I can at least pretend to relax.

BRADLEY: What would you like to drink, darling?

ANN: (*Crossing to close the curtains*) After almost fifty years of marriage, you know very well what I'd like.

BRADLEY: After almost fifty years of marriage, I know very well always to ask.

ANN: Then I'd like a very dry martini, with plenty of ice . . .

ANN & BRADLEY: . . . and a small twist of lemon.

BRADLEY: Thy will be done.
(HE *goes to the bar, mixes the drink carefully for her.*)

ANN: (*To* JOHN, *after* SHE *has partially pulled the curtains*) Don't ask me when we'll eat. We are flying on a wing and a prayer in the dinner department.

JOHN: Who've you got out there, Mother? Mildred? Agnes? Who?

ANN: Neither one. Mildred has broken her hip, and Agnes has gone to meet her maker.

JOHN: Aw . . .

ANN: What I have, out there, is Agnes's cousin's niece, who arrived in a snappy red convertible, and whose name is Cheryl Marie, and who I suspect has never made gravy in her life.

JOHN: We should have just made dinner ourselves, Mother.

ANN: Oh yes. "Ourselves." I've heard that one before. "Ourselves" . . . "Ourselves" means me. It means that yours truly is slaving away out there while the rest of you are enjoying the cocktail hour in here. No thank you, John. I believe in paying people to do things occasionally, even if the person paid happens to be named Cheryl Marie.
(SHE *sits on the couch.*)

BRADLEY: *(Handing her a drink)* Here you are, darling.

ANN: Thank you, dear.
(To JOHN*)*
No, I'm sorry. The cocktail hour is sacred, in my humble opinion. Even when your father and I are home alone, we still have it. In the kitchen. While I'm cooking.
(SHE *holds out her hand automatically for a cocktail napkin.*)

BRADLEY: *(Handing her a stack of cocktail napkins)* That's why we did the kitchen over. So we could have it in there.

ANN: I know you children all think you're too busy to have it.

BRADLEY: You're missing something.

ANN: I think so, too.

BRADLEY: *(Joining* ANN *on the couch)* We're never too busy for the cocktail hour.

ANN: It allows people to unwind.

BRADLEY: It allows people to sit down together at the end of the day . . .

ANN: To talk things over . . . Settle things down . . .

BRADLEY: The bishop used to say—remember this, darling?— Bishop Dow used to say when he came here for dinner that the cocktail hour took the place of evening prayers.

ANN: Well, I don't know about that.

BRADLEY: No, he did. That's what he said.

ANN: Well, all I know is I cherish it. And now I want to know what I've already missed.

JOHN: Nothing.

BRADLEY: We had a brief discussion of the contemporary theater.

JOHN: Which terminated rather abruptly.

ANN: *(Looking from* ONE *to the* OTHER*)* Oh.
(Pause)
   Who'll have some brie? Bradley?

BRADLEY: No, thank you.

ANN: John?

JOHN: *(Pulling up a footstool)* Thanks.

ANN: I must say I love the theater.

BRADLEY: Used to love it.

ANN: It used to be very much a part of our lives.

BRADLEY: Years ago. Before the Erlanger Theatre was torn down.

ANN: All the plays would come here.

BRADLEY: All the good plays.

JOHN: I remember . . .

ANN: Such wonderful plays. With such wonderful plots. They were always about these attractive couples . . .

BRADLEY: And the husband would have committed some minor indiscretion . . .

ANN: Normally the wife did, darling.

BRADLEY: No, no. I think it was he . . .

ANN: She did it more, sweetie. The *wife* was normally the naughty one.

BRADLEY: Well, whoever it was, they were all very attractive about it. And they'd have these attractive leading ladies . . .

ANN: Gertrude Lawrence, Ina Claire, Katharine Hepburn . . .

BRADLEY: They'd all come here . . .

JOHN: I remember your talking about them . . .

BRADLEY: Your mother played tennis with Hepburn at the Tennis Club.

ANN: Oh, I think we hit a ball or two . . .

BRADLEY: Your mother beat her.

ANN: Oh, I don't think I *beat* her, Bradley.

BRADLEY: You beat Katharine Hepburn, my love.

ANN: I think we might have played a little doubles, darling.

BRADLEY: You beat Hepburn, six-three, six-four! *That* I remember!

ANN: Well, maybe I did.

BRADLEY: And we met the Lunts.

ANN: Oh, the Lunts, the Lunts . . .

BRADLEY: They were friends of Bill Hart's. So we all met at the Statler for a cocktail. After a matinee.

ANN: They were terribly amusing.

JOHN: I remember your telling me about the Lunts.

BRADLEY: They could both talk at exactly the same time . . . (THEY do this, of course.)

ANN: Without interrupting each other . . .

BRADLEY: It was uncanny . . .

ANN: They'd say the wittiest things . . .

BRADLEY: Simultaneously . . .

ANN: And you'd understand both . . .

BRADLEY: It was absolutely uncanny.

ANN: Of course they'd been married so long . . .

BRADLEY: Knew each other so well . . .

ANN: They made you feel very sophisticated.
(THEY BOTH *unconsciously cross their legs at the same time*)

BRADLEY: *(Touching her hand)* They made you feel proud to be married.

ANN: Absolutely. I totally agree.
(Pause)
I wish you'd write plays like that, John.

BRADLEY: Won't do it. Refuses to. Simply doesn't want to.

ANN: But I mean, there's a real *need*. Jane Babcock went to Connecticut last weekend to visit her old roommate from Westover, and they thought they'd go into New York to see a play. Well, they looked in the paper and there was absolutely nothing they wanted to see. Finally, they decided to take a chance on one of those noisy English musicals. But when they called for tickets, the man said he was going to charge them three dollars extra. Just for telephoning. When they were calling long distance anyway. Well, that did it, of course. They went to the movies instead. And apparently the movie was perfectly horrible. People were shooting each other—in the *face*, and using the most repulsive language while they were doing it, and the audience was composed of noisy teenagers who screamed and yelled and rattled candy wrappers all around them. Finally they walked out and drove back to New Canaan, thoroughly disappointed with each other and the world. Jane said they really didn't snap out of it until they had cocktails.

BRADLEY: It's all over. The life we led is completely gone.

ANN: Jane said if one of your plays had been on, John, they would have gone to that. And paid the extra three dollars, too.

JOHN: *(Glancing at* BRADLEY*)* My plays are a sore subject, Mother.

ANN: Oh dear.

BRADLEY: A very sore subject.

ANN: Yes, well, it seems that John at least makes some attempt to write about things we know.

BRADLEY: Oh yes. Undercutting, trivializing . . .

ANN: Oh now, darling . . .

BRADLEY: *(Looking warily at manuscript)* What's it called, this play?

JOHN: It's called *The Cocktail Hour*, actually.

BRADLEY: It's called the *what*?

JOHN: *The Cocktail Hour.*

BRADLEY: That's a terrible title.

ANN: Oh now, sweetheart . . .

BRADLEY: Terrible.

JOHN: Why is it terrible?

BRADLEY: To begin with, it's been used.

JOHN: That's *The Cocktail PARTY*, Pop. That's T. S. Eliot.

BRADLEY: Even worse. We walked out on that one.

ANN: This is *The Cocktail HOUR*, darling.

BRADLEY: Doesn't make any difference.

ANN: No, it does. A cocktail *party* is a public thing. You *invite* people to a cocktail party. A cocktail *hour* is family. It's private. It's personal. It's very different.

BRADLEY: Nobody will know that. It will confuse everyone. They'll come expecting T. S. Eliot, and they'll get John. Either way, they'll want their money back.

JOHN: They won't want anything back, Pop. I'm putting it on the shelf. Remember?

ANN: On the shelf?

BRADLEY: Where I hope it will remain for a very long time.

ANN: Is that the solution?

BRADLEY: That's the solution. We've agreed on that. That's what we've agreed on.
(HE *goes into the hall to check the barometer.*)

ANN: Oh dear.
(Pause)
How's Ellen, by the way?

JOHN: Fine.

ANN: I wish she had come along.

JOHN: She had a conference today, Mother.

ANN: Oh, I think that's wonderful. I wish I'd had a job when I was young.

BRADLEY: *(From the hall)* All changing, all going . . .

ANN: And how are the children?

JOHN: Fine. Getting on. Growing up. Charlie already plans to go all the way out to the University of Colorado.

BRADLEY: All gone . . . Married couples leading totally different lives. Children scattered all over the map . . .

ANN: I wish you'd brought them all along.

BRADLEY: *(Returning to the room)* I wish Jigger had come.

ANN: I wish everyone had come. John's family, Jigger's . . .

BRADLEY: We could have made this a family reunion.

JOHN: Which is another play by T. S. Eliot.

BRADLEY: *(Crossing to piano)* I don't care about that. All I know is that if Jigger had come, we'd be gathered around that piano right now. We'd be singing all the old songs: *Kiss Me, Kate—Southern Pacific . . .*

JOHN: It's *"South" Pacific*, Pop.

BRADLEY: Whatever it is, Jigger could play it. I miss him. I miss him terribly.

ANN: We miss *all* the family, Bradley. Everyone.

BRADLEY: Yes. That's right. Of course.
(To JOHN, *indicating the photographs on the piano)*
You have that lovely wife, you have those fine, strapping children, do you ever write about them? Do you ever write about how hard your wife has worked over those children? Do you ever tell how your son pitched a no-hitter in Little League? How your sweet Elsie won the art prize? Do you ever write about your brother winning the Sailing Cup? Do we ever hear anything good in your plays? Oh no. Instead you attack your parents in their old age.

JOHN: It's not an *attack*, Pop.

ANN: *(Quickly)* What if you turned it into a book, John? Books aren't quit so public. Billy Leeming wrote some book about *his* parents, and our local bookstores didn't even bother to carry it. Is it all right if he puts us in a book, Bradley?

JOHN: I can't write it as a book.

ANN: You can certainly try.
(To BRADLEY*)*
It seems a shame to waste all that work.

BRADLEY: *(Looking out a window)* Where's Nina? Where's our daughter? She's normally right on time.

ANN: I think she had to do something with Portia. She'll be here. Meanwhile, I'd like another drink, Bradley. A weak one—but nonetheless, another.

JOHN: I'll get it.

ANN: No, your father likes to get it.

BRADLEY: While I still can.
(HE bends over to get her glass with some difficulty.)

JOHN: Your back O.K., Pop?

ANN: He's got a pinched nerve.

BRADLEY: Your mother thinks it's a pinched nerve.

ANN: Dr. Randall thinks it's a pinched nerve.

BRADLEY: Well, I think it's something far more serious.

JOHN: What do you think it is, Pop?

BRADLEY: Never mind. We'll call it a pinched nerve because that makes people more comfortable. We'll settle for a pinched nerve.
(HE goes to mix ANN's drink.)

ANN: *(Silently mouthing the words to JOHN)* It's a pinched nerve.

BRADLEY: *(Mixing her drink)* And when I was in the hospital with double pneumonia, it was just a cold. I was lying there half-dead with a temperature of one hundred and four, and people would telephone, very much concerned, and your mother would say. "Oh, he's fine, he's perfectly fine, it's just a cold." When they're lowering me into my grave, she'll tell all my friends that it's hay fever.
(HE works on her drink.)

ANN: *(Eying the manuscript)* I suppose I should at least read the thing.

JOHN: Don't if you don't want to.

ANN: Maybe if I read it, it wouldn't seem so frightening.

BRADLEY: Who's frightened? Nobody's frightened.

ANN: Trouble is, it's always so painful, John. Reading your things. And seeing them acted, it's even worse. With all those people *watching*.

BRADLEY: It won't be acted.

ANN: But it should be *done*, Bradley.

BRADLEY: Not this one, please.

ANN: But he's written it. It's his *career.*

BRADLEY: *(As* HE *stirs* ANN's *drink)* It's not his career. Publishing is his career. That's what's paid the bills and brought up those children. That, and considerable help from you and me. What we're talking about here is an amusing little hobby which probably costs more than it brings in. Which is fine. We all have hobbies. I like my golf. I like to travel. But I don't use my hobby to attack my parents or make them look foolish in the eyes of the world.
*(*ANN *finally gets her drink out of his hands.)*

JOHN: It's not a hobby! And I don't attack!

BRADLEY: Well, I don't care. I don't want to be on some stage. I don't want to have some actor imitating me. I've got very little time left on this earth . . .

ANN: Oh, Bradley . . .

BRADLEY: Very little. Much less than anyone thinks.

ANN: Now stop that, Bradley.

BRADLEY: And I don't want people laughing at me, or critics commenting about me, or the few friends I have left commiserating with me in these final days. I don't want that, John. I'm sorry. No.
*(*HE *crosses to sit in his chair.)*

ANN: One thing, John. If you don't do it, you won't get your name in the paper. And that's a good thing, in my humble opinion. I've never liked the publicity which appears with plays. It always seemed slightly cheap to me.

BRADLEY: Of course it is.

ANN: And it's dangerous. People read your name, and think you're rich, and rob you. Peggy Fentriss had her name in the paper for her work with the Philharmonic, and when she went to Bermuda, these burglars backed up a whole truck. They even took a grapefruit she left in the refrigerator.

BRADLEY: *(Suddenly)* What do you stand to lose if you don't put this thing on?

JOHN: *(Ironically)* Just my life, that's all, Pop. Just my life.

BRADLEY: Money. I'm talking about money. How much money would you make on it?

JOHN: You can't tell, Pop.

BRADLEY: Give me an educated guess.

JOHN: Oh . . . A little. If we're lucky.

BRADLEY: "A little. If we're lucky." What kind of an answer is that? No wonder you never went into business.

JOHN: I don't *know*, Pop.

ANN: I don't see why we have to talk about money, Bradley.

BRADLEY: What's the average amount of money you've made on your other plays?

JOHN: Average?

BRADLEY: Give me an average amount . . . Five thousand? Ten? What?

JOHN: Pop . . .

BRADLEY: *(Crossing to the desk)* I will give you a check for twenty thousand dollars right now for not putting on that play.

ANN: Bradley!

BRADLEY: Twenty thousand dollars . . .
(HE *sits down at the desk, finds his checkbook, makes out a check.*)

JOHN: Oh, Pop . . .

ANN: *(Putting down her drink)* Twenty *thousand*!

BRADLEY: You can't cash it, of course, till Monday, till I've covered it from savings, but I am hereby giving you a check.

JOHN: I don't want a check.

BRADLEY: Well, you might as well take it, because if you don't, I'll simply leave you twenty thousand extra in my will.

ANN: Oh, Bradley, now stop it!

BRADLEY: *(Holding out the check to* JOHN*)* Here. It's a good deal. You'll be twenty thousand to the good, and you can still put the thing on after I'm dead.

JOHN: *(Walking away from it)* Pop, I can't . . .

BRADLEY: *(Following him)* And if you invest it, you'll have the interest besides, which you wouldn't have otherwise.

ANN: I can't stand this.

JOHN: I don't want that money, Pop!

BRADLEY: And I don't want that play! I want some peace and privacy in the few days I have left of my life. And I'm willing to pay for it. Now there it is.
(Puts the check on the table by his chair.)
If you have any business sense at all, you'll take it. And if you don't want it for yourself, then give it to your children, who I hope will show more respect for you in your old age than you've ever shown for me.

JOHN: Oh, Pop, oh, Pop, oh, Pop . . .
(NINA'S VOICE *is heard from the hall.*)

NINA'S VOICE: Hello!

ANN: Ah. There's Nina. *(Calling off)* We're having cocktails, dear! *(To* OTHERS*).* I think it might be time to change the subject.
*(*NINA *enters, well-dressed, attractive, mid-forties, removing her raincoat.)*

NINA: *(Kissing her* MOTHER*)* I'm terribly sorry I'm late. Portia's in trouble again.

ANN: Oh no.

JOHN: Who's Portia?

NINA: *(Kissing her* FATHER*)* She was up all night, wandering from room to room, sighing and groaning.

ANN: Oh no.

BRADLEY: That sweet Portia.

JOHN: Who's Portia?

NINA: And we also think there's something radically wrong with her rear end.
*(*SHE *tosses her raincoat on the banister.)*

ANN: Oh no.

BRADLEY: Poor thing.

JOHN: Who the hell is *Portia*?

NINA: *(Kissing her* BROTHER*)* Portia is our new golden retriever, and we're very worried about her.

BRADLEY: Portia is a brilliant beast. You should write a play about Portia.

JOHN: I could call it *Practical Dogs*. As opposed to *Practical Cats*. By T. S. Eliot.

BRADLEY: What would you like to drink, Pookins?

NINA: Just white wine, please.

JOHN: I'll get it, Pop.

BRADLEY: *(Crossing to bar)* *I'll* get it. I'm still capable of officiating at my own bar.

NINA: Plenty of rocks, please. And plenty of soda water. My stomach is in absolute knots.

JOHN: Over Portia?

BRADLEY: Portia is superb. I adore Portia.

NINA: Over everything.

ANN: Poor Nina, and her nervous stomach.

NINA: Let's not talk about my stomach, Mother. Let's talk about John. I hear you've written another play, John. *(Sitting on the couch)*

BRADLEY: We're not discussing it.

NINA: Why not?

ANN: It's a sore subject.

NINA: Why?

ANN: Apparently it's primarily about you-know-who.

NINA: Oh. *(Pause.* SHE *sees it on the coffee table.)* Is that it?

ANN: That's it. *(*NINA *gingerly lifts the cover and looks inside.)*

NINA: *(Reading) The Cocktail Hour.* Hmmm.

BRADLEY: Stupid title.

NINA: They'll confuse it with Eliot.

BRADLEY: Exactly, Pookins.

NINA: Is it going on?

BRADLEY: No.

ANN: Maybe not.

JOHN: I came up to ask his permission.

BRADLEY: And I said no.

NINA: Hmmm.

BRADLEY: *(Bringing her a glass of wine)* Here's your wine, darling.

NINA: Thank you. *(Pause)* Is Mother in it?

ANN: Apparently I am.

NINA: Is Jigger?

BRADLEY: I hope not.
(HE *sits in his chair.)*

JOHN: Well, he is. In a way.

NINA: Are you in it, John?

JOHN: I'm afraid I am.

BRADLEY: I think we've said enough on the subject. I want to know where Ed is, Pookins. I thought Ed would be with you.

NINA: Ed's in New York. On business for the bank.

BRADLEY: I see. Well, we'll miss him.

ANN: *(Now doing her needlepoint)* Oh yes. We'll miss Ed.

NINA: *(To* JOHN*)* Am I in it?

JOHN: I think Pop wants us to change the subject.

BRADLEY: Thank you, John.

NINA: I just want to know if I'm *in* it.

JOHN: Yes, you are.

NINA: Oh God.

BRADLEY: Tell us about the children, Pookins. I want to hear about my grandchildren.

NINA: They're all fine, Pop.
(SHE *picks up script, holds it to her ear.*)

ANN: What are you doing, dear?

NINA: I think I heard this thing ticking.

ANN: *(Laughing)* That's funny.

NINA: Do you think we should drop it in a big bucket of water?

BRADLEY: I think we should change the subject. Tell me about Andy. Does he like his job?

NINA: *(Putting script down)* He likes it fine, Pop.
(*To* JOHN, *as* SHE *thumbs through the script.*)
I hate to think what you do to me in this thing.

JOHN: You come out all right.

NINA: I'll bet. Am I the wicked older sister?

JOHN: No.

NINA: Am I the uptight, frustrated, bossy bitch?

JOHN: No, no.

NINA: Well, what am I, then?

JOHN: Actually, you play a relatively minor role.

ANN: Sounds like you're lucky, dear.

BRADLEY: Tell me about Wendy. Is Wendy doing well at Williams? Does she still want to be in business?

NINA: Do I get a *name*, at least? What's my name here?

JOHN: I call you Diana.

ANN: Diana?

JOHN: *(To* NINA*)* Isn't that what you used to wish your name was? The Goddess Diana, Protectress of Wild Animals.

ANN: I knew a Diana Finch once. She used to climb down drainpipes and hang around drugstores. No, I don't like the name.

NINA: Well, it's better than *Nina*, Mother. Which means little Ann. Little you. Sweet little carbon copy.

BRADLEY: I asked you a question about Wendy, Pookins.

NINA: *(Impatiently)* She's fine, Pop.
*(*SHE *continues to thumb.)*
I only see about ten pages of Diana here.
(More thumbing)
And in the second act, less than that.

JOHN: It's what's known as a supporting role.

NINA: Supporting? What do I support?

ANN: I imagine all of us, dear. You give us all support. Which is true.

BRADLEY: May we talk about something else?

NINA: Do I get to bring in trays? Or do I just carry a spear?

JOHN: You come and go.

NINA: Come and go? Mostly go. I'd say, thank you very much.
(Reads)
"Diana exits huffily." Oh, boy there it is. "Huffily." Jesus, John.
*(*SHE *gets up huffily.)*

BRADLEY: All right, then.
*(*HE *goes to the bookcase, gets a large volume—Life's Pictured History of World War II—and takes it to a chair in the front hall where* HE *begins to thumb through it determinedly.)*
While all of you continue to concentrate on one very tiresome subject, I will try to exercise my mind. Let me know, please, if, as, and when you're willing to broaden the discussion.
*(*HE *turns his back on the* GROUP.*)*

NINA: I just think it's interesting. I always play a minor role in this family.

ANN: That's not true, darling.

JOHN: You were the one who always owned the dogs.

ANN: We gave you that lovely coming-out party.

JOHN: You got that trip to Europe.

ANN: You had the most beautiful wedding . . .

BRADLEY: *(From the hall)* You got my mother's tea set after she died, Pookins.

JOHN: Jigger and I used to call you the Gravy Train Girl.

NINA: Well, not any more, apparently.

ANN: Maybe you're lucky to get off the hook, dear.

NINA: Oh boy, John. I swear. It's the old story. Once again, you and Jigger, who never show up here, who come up once a year for a day or two, *if* we're lucky, when we have to drop everything we're doing and rush to be at your beck and call—once again, you two end up getting all the attention, whereas I, I, who have remained here since I was married, who have lived here all my *life* . . . who see Mother and Pop at least once a week, who have them for Christmas and Thanksgiving and even *Easter*, for God's sake . . . I, who got Pop to go to a younger doctor . . . I, me, who drove Mother all over town for *weeks* after her cataract operation . . . who found them a new cleaning woman when their old one just walked *out*! . . . once again I am told I play a goddamn minor ROLE!

ANN: Now, now . . . Now, now.

BRADLEY: *(From the hall)* You've been a wonderful daughter, Pookins.

NINA: *(Crossing to the bar)* Wonderful or not, I need another drink.

ANN: Be careful, darling. Your stomach.

NINA: Oh, what difference does that make? Who cares? I just play a minor role. If I get ulcers, they're minor ulcers. If I die, it's a minor death.

JOHN: Nina, hey, lookit. I kept trying to build up your part.

NINA: I'll bet.

JOHN: I did. But I never got anywhere.

NINA: Why not?

JOHN: I never could get your number.

BRADLEY: *(From the hall)* I don't know why anybody has to get anybody else's number.

JOHN: No, I mean, you always seem so content around here.

NINA: Con*tent*?

JOHN: Good husband. Good kids. Good life. You always came out seeming so comfortable and at home.

BRADLEY: *(From the hall)* I should damn well hope so.

NINA: *Me*? Is this *me* you're talking about? Comfortable and at home?

ANN: He's giving you a compliment, dear.

NINA: Is he? Is that a compliment? Comfortable and at home? Oh boy, that's a laugh. That's a good one, John. Boy, you've really painted me into a corner. Ask Dr. Randall how comfortable I am. Ask him to show you the X-rays of my insides. He'll show you what it's like to be at home.

BRADLEY: *(Coming back in)* Pookins, sweetheart . . .

NINA: *(Revving up)* Do you know anything about my *life*, John? Have you ever bothered to inquire what I *do* around here, all these years you've been away? Did you know I am vice-president of the S.P.C.A.?

ANN: *And* on the hospital board. *And* the School for the Blind. *And* the gift shop at the gallery . . .

NINA: Did you know that I am interested in seeing-eye *dogs*, John? Did you know that? I am profoundly interested in them. I'm good with dogs, I'm the best, everyone says that, and what I want to do more than anything else in the world is go to this two-year school in Cleveland where you do nothing but work with seeing-eye dogs.

ANN: You can't just commute to Cleveland, darling.

NINA: I *know* that, Mother.

JOHN: Why can't you?

NINA: Because I have a husband, John. Because I have a— *life*!

BRADLEY: And a very good life it is, Pookins.

NINA: I mean, what am I supposed to *do*, John? Start subsidizing Eastern Airlines every other *day*? Live in some mo*tel*? Rattle around some strange city where I don't know a *soul*? Just because I want to work with . . . because I happen to feel an attachment to . . . oh God. *(SHE starts to cry.)*

BRADLEY: *(Going to her)* Oh now, Pookins . . . Now stop, sweetie pie . . .

ANN: I didn't realize people could get quite so upset about dogs.

BRADLEY: It's not dogs, it's John.
(Wheeling on JOHN)
You see what happens? You arrive here and within half an hour, you've thrown the whole family into disarray. It's happened all your life. Par for the course, my friend. Par for the course.
(Comforting NINA)
Now calm down, sweetheart. He's not going to do the play anyway.

NINA: *(Breaking away)* Well, he should! He should do one about *me*! You've never written about me, John. Ever. Why don't you, some time? Why don't you write about a woman who went to the right schools, and married the right man, and lived on the right street all the days of her life, and ended up feeling perfectly terrible!
(SHE *runs out of the room and upstairs.)*

BRADLEY: There you are, John. You satisfied? Will you put that in your play? Or do you still want to concentrate all your guns on your dying father?
(HE *goes out after* NINA, *calling)*
Wait, Nina. Pookins. Sweetheart . . .
(HE *follows her Off and upstairs. Pause.)*

ANN: *(Holding out her glass)* I might have just a splash more, John.

JOHN: *(Taking her glass)* O.K., Mother.

ANN: Just a splash. I'm serious.

JOHN: *(Mixing it)* Right.

ANN: You're not having anything?

JOHN: Can't seem to get away with it these days, Mother.

ANNe: What does that mean?

JOHN: Very quickly, I turn into an angry drunk.

ANN: Good heavens. Why is that?

JOHN: I don't know . . .
(Looks where his FATHER *has gone.)*
I guess I'm sore about something. *(Pause)* Is he as sick as he says he is, Mother?

ANN: You know your father.

JOHN: He keeps saying he's dying.

ANN: He's been saying that for years. He announced it on his fortieth birthday. He reminds us of it whenever he gets a cold. Lately, when we go to bed, he doesn't say "goodnight" any more. He says, "goodbye," because he thinks he won't last till morning.

JOHN: But you think he's O.K.?

ANN: I think . . . No, I *know*, we all know, that he has a blood problem, a kind of leukemia, which seems to be in remission now. Somehow I don't think that will kill him. Something else will.

JOHN: You think my play will?

ANN: *He* seems to think it will.

JOHN: Oh God . . .

ANN: And *you* must think it might, John. Otherwise you never would have bothered to clear it with him.

JOHN: I almost wish I hadn't.

ANN: I'm glad you did. It shows you have strong family feelings.

JOHN: Family feelings, family feelings! The story of my life! The bane of my existence! Family feelings. Dear Mother, dear Pop. May I have permission to cross the street? May I have permission to buy a car? Would you mind very much if I screwed my girl?

ANN: Now that's enough of that, please.

JOHN: Well, it's true! Family feelings. May I have your approval to put on a play? Oh God, why did I come here? Why did I bother? Most playwrights dish out the most brutal diatribes against their parents, who sit proudly in the front row and applaud every insult that comes along. Me? Finally—after fifteen years of beating around the bush—I come up with something which is—all right, maybe a little on the nose, maybe a little frank, maybe a little satiric at times—but still clearly infused with warmth, respect, and an abiding affection, and what happens? I'm being censored, banned, bribed not to produce.

ANN: I still wish you'd make it a book.

JOHN: Oh, Mother . . .

ANN: No, I'm serious. Books are quieter.

JOHN: I can't write books.

ANN: You work on them all the time.

JOHN: But I can't write them.

ANN: Plays are so noisy.

JOHN: I know.

ANN: They cause such attention.

JOHN: I know.

ANN: I don't mean just for us. I mean for you, as well.

JOHN: I know, Mother.

ANN: Those reviews must hurt terribly. The bad ones.

JOHN: They do.

ANN: All coming out together. Wave after wave. Every little suburban newspaper putting in its two-cents worth. And they can all be so mean.

JOHN: Right.

ANN: Book reviewers seem kinder, somehow. You have the feeling that people who write books get their friends to review them.

JOHN: Yes . . .

ANN: But not with plays. I mean, who *are* those people who review plays? What do they do when they're not sitting around criticizing?

JOHN: I hear some of them are decent folks, Mother.

ANN: They well may be, but I don't think they have the faintest notion what you're writing about.

JOHN: Sometimes they don't seem to.

ANN: They don't like us, John. They resent us. They think we're all Republicans, and all superficial, and all alcoholics.

JOHN: I know.

ANN: *(Taking a sip; with a twinkle)* Only the latter is true. *(*JOHN *laughs, possibly hugs her.)*
I also think . . .

JOHN: What?

ANN: Never mind.

JOHN: No, come on, Mother. What?

ANN: I also think he's scared you'll spill the beans.

JOHN: The beans?

ANN: The beans.

JOHN: What beans?

ANN: Oh, John, face it. Everyone's got beans to spill. And, knowing you, you'll find a way to spill ours.

JOHN: I'm simply trying to tell the truth, Mother.

ANN: Fine. Good. But tell the truth in a *book*. Books take their time. Books *explain* things. If you have to do this, do it quietly and carefully in a book.

JOHN: I can't, Mother.

ANN: You can try.

JOHN: I *can't*. Maybe I'm a masochist, but I can't seem to write anything but plays. I can't write movies or television. I'm caught, I'm trapped in this old medium. It's artificial, it's archaic, it's restrictive beyond belief. It doesn't seem to have anything to do with contemporary American life. I feel like some medieval stonecutter, hacking away in the dark corner of an abandoned monastery, while everyone else is outside, having fun in the Renaissance. And when I finish, a few brooding inquisitors shuffle gloomily in, take a quick look, and say,

"That's not it. That's not what we want at all!" Oh, God, why do I do it? Why write plays? Why are they the one thing in the world I want to do? Why have I always done them?

ANN: Not always, John. You used to write the most marvelous letters, for example. From camp. From boarding school . . .

JOHN: But I wrote plays long before that. Long before I could even write, I put on plays.

ANN: Oh well. Those things you did down in the playroom.

JOHN: They were *plays*, Mother. I'd clear the electric trains off the Ping-Pong table so it could be a stage. And I'd use up all the crayons in the house doing the scenery. And use up all my allowance bribing Nina and Jigger to be in them.

ANN: And then you'd drag your father and me down and we'd have to sit through the damn things.

JOHN: But they were plays, Mother.

ANN: Yes. I suppose they were.

JOHN: What were they about, Mother? Do you remember?

ANN: I do not.

JOHN: My psychiatrist keeps asking me what they were about. He says they could open a few doors for me, but I've blocked them all.

ANN: I wish you'd block that psychiatrist.

JOHN: But if there was a pattern to the plots, if there was some common theme to what I was doing, it would . . .

ANN: It would what?

JOHN: Explain things . . . I wish you could remember.
(Pause)

ANN: You always gave yourself a leading part, I remember that.

JOHN: I'll bet.

ANN: And it seems to me you always played this foundling, this outsider, this adopted child . . .

JOHN: Is that true?

ANN: I think so. Your father and I would roll our eyes and think, what have we wrought. I mean, on you'd come, this poor prince who'd been adopted by beggars. Or else . . .

JOHN: What?

ANN: I remember one particularly silly one. You were the court jester. You put on a bathing suit and a red bathing cap and started dancing around, being very fresh.

JOHN: Hold it. Say that again. What did I wear?

ANN: You wore your little wool bathing trunks from Best and Company, and Nina's red bathing camp.

JOHN: *The Red-Headed Dummy.*

ANN: I suppose.

JOHN: No, I mean that was the title of my play: *The Red-Headed Dummy!* It's coming back!

ANN: Well, whatever it was, I remember it went on for-*ever*! It made us late for dinner somewhere.

JOHN: Good God, Mother, I suddenly realize what I was doing in that play.

ANN: Well, *I* certainly don't.

JOHN: I think I know! And I think my shrink would agree!

ANN: I'm all ears.

JOHN: It's a little Freudian, Mother. It's a little raw.

ANN: Then I'm not terribly interested. *(Pause)* What?

JOHN: What I was doing was parading my penis in front of my parents.

ANN: Oh, John, honestly.

JOHN: I was! The bathing suit, the red cap, *The Red-Headed Dummy!* Get it? I was doing a phallic dance.

ANN: John, don't be unattractive.

JOHN: No, no, really. I was playing my own penis. Smart kid, come to think of it. How many guys in the world get a chance to do that? Especially in front of their parents.

ANN: I think it's time to turn to another topic.

JOHN: No, but wait. Listen, Mother. I'll put it in a historical context. What I was doing was acting out a basic, primitive impulse which goes back to the Greeks. That's how comedy *originated*, Mother! The phallic dance! These peasants would do these gross dances in front of their overlords to see what they could get away with! And that's what I was doing, too, at three-years-old! Me! The Red-Headed Dummy! Dancing under the noses of my parents, before they went out to dinner! Saying, "Hey, you guys. Look. Look over here. I'm here, I'm alive, I'm wild, I have this penis with a mind of its own!" That's what I was doing then! That's what I've always done! That's what I'm doing right now, right in this room! And that's why I have to write plays, Mother. I have to keep doing it.
(Long pause)

ANN: Are you finished, John?

JOHN: For now, at least.

ANN: All right, then, I want to say this: I don't like all this psychological talk, John. I never have. I think it's cheap and self-indulgent. I've never liked the fact that you've consulted a psychiatrist, and your father agrees with me. It upsets us very much to think that the money we give you at Christmas goes for paying that person rather than for taking your children to Aspen or somewhere. I don't like psychiatrists in general. Celia Underwood went to one, and now she bursts into tears whenever she plays bridge. Psychiatrists make you think about yourself too much. And about the bedroom too much. There's no need!

JOHN: Mother—

ANN: No, please let me finish. Now I want you to write, John. I think sometimes you write quite well, and I think it's a healthy enterprise. But I think you should write *books*. In books, you can talk the way you've just talked and it's not embarrassing. In books, you can go into people's minds . . . Now we all have things in our lives which we've done, or haven't done, which a book could make clear. I mean, I myself could tell you . . . I could tell you . . . I could tell you lots of things if I knew you would write them down quietly and carefully and sympathetically in a good, long book . . .

(BRADLEY enters.)

BRADLEY: What book?

ANN: We were just talking about the value of a good book, dear.

BRADLEY: *(Crossing to his chair)* I agree with you. I'm reading the Bible now, John. I keep it right by my bed. It's surprisingly good reading. And excellent insurance.

ANN: How's Nina? And where's Nina?

BRADLEY: Nina is fine. Nina is dealing with a slight confusion in the kitchen.

ANN: *(Jumping up)* I knew it. I could feel it in my bones. Tell me what happened.

BRADLEY: There was a slight misunderstanding about the oven.

ANN: Explain that, please.

BRADLEY: The oven was inadvertently turned off.

ANN: You mean that beautiful roast of beef . . .

BRADLEY: Is at the moment somewhat underdone.

ANN: Oh, I could cry.

BRADLEY: Now don't *worry*, darling. The oven is now working overtime. And there's even talk of Yorkshire pudding.

ANN: How can that creature make Yorkshire pudding if she can't cook a simple roast?

BRADLEY: Because I asked her to, darling. And because I presented her with another package of peas from the deep freeze.

ANN: Why more peas? What happened to the peas she had?

BRADLEY: I'm afraid there was a lack of attention to the right rear burner, darling.

ANN: Oh, I can't *stand* this! We'll be lucky if we eat by nine! I should have known never to take a chance on someone named Cheryl Marie!
(SHE *hurries out, ad-libbing about the roast beef*)

BRADLEY: *(Calling after her)* Her name is Sharon, dear. *Sharon* Marie.
(Pause; to JOHN*)* Do you have any servants in this play of yours?

JOHN: Not really.

BRADLEY: "Not really"? What does that mean, "Not really"? Does your producer have to pay for a maid or not?

JOHN: No, he doesn't, Pop.

BRADLEY: Probably just as well. Knowing you, you'd get them all wrong anyway.

JOHN: Thanks.

BRADLEY: Well, I mean, nobody understands how to treat servants today. Even your mother. She was born with them, they brought her breakfast in bed until she married me, and I'm afraid she takes them too much for granted. Your generation is worse. You don't even seem to know they're there. Now I went out just now and spoke personally to Sharon Marie. I inquired about her life. And because I took the time to converse with her, because I made her feel part of the family, you may be sure we will have a much more delicious dinner.

JOHN: And because you tipped her twenty bucks.

BRADLEY: Yes. All right. I did that, too. Because I firmly believe good service is important. You can't live without servants. At least you can't live well. Civilization depends on them. They are the mainstay of intelligent life. Without them, you and I would be out in the kitchen right now, slicing onions and shouting over the Dispose-All, and none of this would be taking place at all.

JOHN: You're probably right.

BRADLEY: Of course I'm right. *(Pause)* I did something else while I was out there, besides buttering up Sharon Marie.

JOHN: What else did you do?

BRADLEY: I put in a call to your brother.

JOHN: Ah.

BRADLEY: Couldn't get him, of course. He's still with a client. Seven-thirty on a Saturday night. Yes, well, we all have to work. We all have to put our shoulder to the wheel. No substitute for good hard work. When the head of General Motor dies, they hire a new office boy.

JOHN: You think that's true, Pop?

BRADLEY: Of course it's true. Or was, until your friend Roosevelt came along and gave everyone a free ride.

JOHN: Hey, now wait a minute . . .

BRADLEY: I can't discuss it. Anyway, I spoke to Sylvia. She expects Jigger home any minute, and then he'll call.

JOHN: Good.

BRADLEY: So when he calls, we can all talk to Jigger. If we can't gather around a piano, we can still gather around a telephone.

JOHN: Fine.
(BRADLEY *goes to the bar to make himself another drink.*)

BRADLEY: I wish you'd have a drink.

JOHN: No thanks, Pop.

BRADLEY: It will still be quite a while before we eat.

JOHN: I can last.

BRADLEY: *(As* HE *makes his drink)* I hate to drink alone.

JOHN: That's O.K.

BRADLEY: As you know, I have very firm rules about alcohol. Never drink before six. Never drink after dinner. And never drink alone. You make me feel like an old souse.

JOHN: I'll have wine, then, Pop.

BRADLEY: Good. It's a convivial thing, drinking together. Even if it's just white wine.

JOHN: Have you got any red there, Pop?

BRADLEY: Red?

JOHN: I don't like white that much.

BRADLEY: You mean I have to go all the way out and open a whole new bottle of red wine?

JOHN: O.K. Pop. A drop of scotch, then.

BRADLEY: *(Reaches for a glass)* A little scotch. *(Pours a strong one)*

JOHN: A *little*, Pop? That looks like a double.

BRADLEY: You can't fly on one wing.

JOHN: Fly? Should I fasten my seat-belt?

BRADLEY: Maybe I just want to have a good, healthy belt with my older son before the evening's over.

JOHN: O.K.
(Raises his glass to his FATHER, *takes a sip. It is obviously strong.)*
Ah.

BRADLEY: *(Looking at the check)* I notice my check is still there.

JOHN: I don't want it, Pop.

BRADLEY: Take it. I insist.

JOHN: I don't want it. *(Pause)*

BRADLEY: *(Settling into his chair)* Tell me a little more about your play.

JOHN: *(On the couch)* It's not going on. I promise.

BRADLEY: I just want to know a little more about it.

JOHN: Pop, we'll just get into trouble . . .

BRADLEY: No, no. We're mature individuals. We're having a drink together at the end of the day . . . For example, does it have a plot?

JOHN: Not much of one, actually.

BRADLEY: I like a good plot.

JOHN: I can't seem to write one.

BRADLEY: I remember learning at Yale: there are three great plots in Western literature: *Oedipus Rex, Tom Jones* and I forget the third.

JOHN: Ben Jonson's *Volpone.*

BRADLEY: No, it wasn't that.

JOHN: According to Coleridge, those are the three great plots.

BRADLEY: No, no.

JOHN: I've just *edited* a textbook on Coleridge, Pop.

BRADLEY: Well, you're still wrong.

JOHN: *(Starts getting up)* I could look it—

BRADLEY: No!

JOHN: O.K.
(Pause. THEY *drink.)*

BRADLEY: So you don't have a plot.

JOHN: Not much of one.

BRADLEY: You don't try to drag in that business about our family having Indian blood, do you?

JOHN: *Do* we?

BRADLEY: We do not. *(Pause)* Though some people keep saying we do.

JOHN: What people?

BRADLEY: Your cousin Wilbur, particularly. He used to bandy it about. But it's an absolute lie. There is no Indian blood in our branch of the family. I want that absolutely understood before I die.

JOHN: O.K.

BRADLEY: Your Great-uncle Ralph may have had a relationship with an Indian woman, but that was it.

JOHN: Did he?

BRADLEY: *May* have. Besides, she was an Indian princess. She was very well-born. According to your grandmother, she was quite beautiful. And she sewed very well.

JOHN: Sowed corn?

BRADLEY: Sewed moccasins. I don't know what she sewed. The point is that Indian blood never came down through our line. Harry Blackburn down at the club constantly brings it up. He says it accounts for our affinity for alcohol. It's not funny, and I told him so, and if he mentions it again, I'm going to punch him in the nose.

JOHN: Take it easy, Pop.

BRADLEY: Anyway, if you bring up that Indian blood stuff in your play, you are simply barking up the wrong tree.

JOHN: I never thought of it, Pop.

BRADLEY: Good.
(HE *crosses to sit next to* JOHN *on the couch.*)
   Did you bring up your grandfather's death?
(*Pause*)

JOHN: Yes.

BRADLEY: I knew you would.

JOHN: I don't make a big deal of it.

BRADLEY: I don't know why you have to make any deal of it at all.

JOHN: I think it helps say who we are.

BRADLEY: You're always harping on it. It seems to be an obsession with you.

JOHN: I just refer to it once, Pop.

BRADLEY: How? What do you say?

JOHN: Oh, well . . .

BRADLEY: I want to know what you say about my father.

JOHN: I say he was a good man, a kind man, one of the best lawyers in town . . .

BRADLEY: True enough . . .

JOHN: A leader in the community. A pillar of the church . . .

BRADLEY: True . . . All true . . .

JOHN: Who, one day, for no discernible reason, strolled down to the edge of the Niagara River, hung his hat, his

coat, and his cane on a wooden piling, and then walked into the water and drowned himself.
(Pause)

BRADLEY: That's what you say in your play?

JOHN: That's what I say, Pop.
(Pause).

BRADLEY: He left a note.

JOHN: I didn't know that, Pop.

BRADLEY: Oh yes. There was a note in his breast pocket. Addressed to me and my mother. I have it in my safe deposit box.

JOHN: I didn't know he left a note.

BRADLEY: You can have it when I die. *(Pause)*
He says there will be enough money to support my mother and to send me through college. *(Pause)* Which there was. *(Pause)* Then he says he's terribly, terribly sorry, but he's come to the conclusion that life isn't worth living any more.
(Pause. BRADLEY turns away from JOHN, takes out a handkerchief and dries his eyes.)

JOHN: Oh, Pop.

BRADLEY: Churchill had those dark moments.

JOHN: So does my son Jack.

BRADLEY: Jack too? That sweet Jack?

JOHN: He gets it in spades.

BRADLEY: Of course, it's just . . . life, isn't it? It's part of the equation. The point is, we don't complain, we deal with it. We divert ourselves. We play golf, we have a drink occasionally.

JOHN: We write plays.

BRADLEY: Well, we do *some*thing. What does that sweet Jack do?

JOHN: Builds model airplanes.

BRADLEY: Oh that poor boy. That poor, poor boy.

JOHN: Yeah, I know.
(Pause)

BRADLEY: And your play gets into all this?

JOHN: A little.

BRADLEY: Sounds like a very depressing play.

JOHN: It has its darker moments.

BRADLEY: But no plot.

JOHN: Not really. No.

BRADLEY: *(Getting up)* Seems to me, you have to have some twist or something. I mean, it's your business, not mine, but it seems to me you need some secret or surprise or something. I thought all plays had to have that.

JOHN: Actually, there is. A little one. At the end of the first act.

BRADLEY: What is it?

JOHN: Oh well.

BRADLEY: Tell it to me.

JOHN: You don't want to hear, Pop.

BRADLEY: Tell it to me anyway.

JOHN: You'll just get angry, Pop.

BRADLEY: I want to hear it. Please.
(Pause)

JOHN: All right. At the end of the first act, I have this older man . . .

BRADLEY: Me. I'm sure it's me.

JOHN: It's you and it's not you, Pop.

BRADLEY: What does this fellow do?

JOHN: He tells his older son . . .

BRADLEY: You.

JOHN: *Partly* me, Pop. Just *partly*.

BRADLEY: Tells his son what?

JOHN: The father tells his son that he doesn't believe . . .

BRADLEY: Doesn't believe what?

JOHN: Doesn't believe his son is his true son.

BRADLEY: WHAT?

JOHN: He says he thinks his wife once had an affair, and the son is the result.

BRADLEY: That is the most ridiculous thing I ever heard in my life!

JOHN: I knew you'd get sore.

BRADLEY: Of course I'm sore. Who wouldn't get sore? Where in God's name did you get such a ridiculous idea?

JOHN: I don't know. It just happened. As I was writing.

BRADLEY: Thank God this play is not going on! It's demeaning to me, and insulting to your mother! Why in heaven's name would you ever want to write a thing like that?

JOHN: Because I don't think you ever loved me, Pop. *(A telephone rings Offstage.)*

BRADLEY: That's Jigger.
(The telephone rings again, as BRADLEY *hurriedly exits Off and up the stairs. Then a half-ring.* BRADLEY'S VOICE *is heard answering from Offstage.)*

BRADLEY'S VOICE: Hello? . . .
*(*JOHN *sits on the couch, looking after his* FATHER, *then looking at his glass.)*

END OF ACT I

ACT II

Immediately after. JOHN *is sitting on the couch. His glass is now empty.* NINA *comes in with a plate of carrot sticks and celery.*

NINA: Here are more munchies. It might be a little while before we eat.

JOHN: What's new with Jigger?

NINA: I don't know. I just had a chance to say hello. But I know how these things work. Mother will get on the phone in their bedroom, and Pop will be on the extension in the guest room, and everyone will talk at once.
*(*SHE *finds her glass.)*
Don't you want to get in on the act?

JOHN: I'll wait till things settle down.

NINA: We're lucky that whoosie out there in the kitchen messed up on the meat. I told her we'll be a minimum of twenty minutes, during which time she can at least *think* about making gravy.

JOHN: You know. I just thought: isn't this familiar?

NINA: What?

JOHN: This. You and me. Sitting here. Stomachs growling. Waiting to eat.

NINA: Because of the cocktail hour . . .

JOHN: Because of Jigger.

NINA: It wasn't always Jigger.

JOHN: Most of the time it was. I was the good little boy, remember? I'd dash home, do my homework, wash my hands, brush my hair, sit here all during cocktails, and then just as we were about to eat, Jigger would call to say that he was still at some game or something.

NINA: Sometimes.

JOHN: All the time. So you'd dig into another one of your Albert Payson Terhune dog books, and Mother and Pop would have another drink and talk about their day, and I'd just sit here stewing.

NINA: That's your problem.

JOHN: Well, it was the maid's problem, too, remember? All those maids, over the years, coming to the doorway in their rustly, starchy uniforms and saying, "Dinner is served, Missus," and Mother would say, "Give us five more minutes, Mabel, or Jean, or Agnes, or whatever your name is this month," but it wouldn't be five, it would be fifteen, it would be half an *hour*, before Jigger got home and our parents would rise from the couch and stagger into the dining room to eat.

NINA: They never staggered, John.

JOHN: No, you're right. They held it beautifully. The cook held dinner beautifully. And the maid kept the plates warm. The cocktail hour kept all of life in an amazing state of suspended animation.

NINA: But oh those meals! Remember those *meals*? Three courses. Soup, a roast, homemade rolls, a homemade dessert! Floating Island, Brown Betty, Pineapple Upside Down Cake . . .

JOHN: Stewed prunes . . .

NINA: Only occasionally. And even that was good!

JOHN: Maybe. But how did those poor souls put up with us night after night? Well, of course, they didn't. They lasted a month or two and then quit, one after the other. We were lucky that one of them didn't appear in the doorway some night with a machine gun and mow us all down!

NINA: Oh, honestly, John. We were good to everyone who worked for us. We'd always go out in the kitchen and make a huge fuss.

JOHN: Oh sure, and cadge an extra cookie while the poor things were trying frantically to clean up. Oh God, Nina, what shits we were about maids!

NINA: We drove them to church, we paid their medical bills . . .
(SHE *takes her shoes off and sprawls on the couch.)*

JOHN: We were shits! When Grandmother died, she left five hundred dollars to each of the three maids that had served her all her life, and the Packard to the chauffeur.

NINA: Mother made it up to them.

JOHN: Oh, sure. She tried. And they tried to make it up to themselves all along the way. Remember the one who stole all that liquor? Or the one who started the fire, smoking in the cedar closet? Or the one who went stark raving made at breakfast and chased Mother around with a butter knife? Oh they had their moments of revenge. But we still built our life on their backs. Has it ever occurred to you that every dinner party, every cocktail hour, good Lord, every civilized endeavor in this world is based on exploiting the labor of the poor Cheryl Maries toiling away offstage.

NINA: Her name is Shirley Marie. *(Pause)* I think. *(Pause)* And she's exploiting *us*. She's probably getting fifty bucks for three hours work, when Mother and I did most of it anyway.

JOHN: There you go. Now we're exploiting each other. Pop always carries on about the importance of civilized life, but think of what it costs to achieve it. Between what Freud tells us we do to ourselves, and what Marx tells us we do to each other, it's a wonder we don't crawl up our own assholes.

NINA: Nicely put, John. All I know is, according to your good wife Ellen, whenever you and she gives a party in New York, you're the first one to want to hire some poor out-of-work actor to serve the soup.

JOHN: Yeah, I know. It's a shitty system, but I can't think of a better one.

NINA: *(Getting up, making another drink)* I think *you're* a shit, John. I'll say that much.

JOHN: What else is new?

NINA: No, I mean now. Tonight. For this.

JOHN: For this?

NINA: Coming up here. Stirring things up. With your play.

JOHN: This is probably one of the most decent things I've ever done.

NINA: Badgering two old people? Threatening them with some ghastly kind of exposure in the last years of their lives?

JOHN: I came here to get their permission.

NINA: You came here to stir things *up*, John. You came here to cause trouble. That's what you've done since the day you were born, and that's what you'll do till you die. You cannot let people alone, can you? A rainy day, a Sunday afternoon, every evening when you finished your homework, off you'd go on your appointed rounds, wandering from room to room in this house, teasing, causing an argument, starting a fight, leaving a trail of upset and unhappy people behind you. And when you finished with all of us, you'd go down in the kitchen and start on the cook. And when the cook left, you'd tease your teachers at school. And now that you're writing plays, you tease the critics! Anyone in authority comes under your guns. Why don't you at least be constructive about it, and tease the Mafia or the C.I.A. for God's sake! (SHE *sits in a chair opposite him.*)

JOHN: Because I'm not a political person.

NINA: Then what kind of person *are* you, John? Why are you so passionately concerned with disturbing the peace? I mean, here we are, the family at least partially together for the first time in several years, and possibly the last time in our lives, and what happens: you torment us with this play, you accuse us of running a slave market in the kitchen, you make us all feel thoroughly uncomfortable. Have you ever thought about this, John? Has it ever come to mind that this is what you do?

JOHN: Yes.

NINA: Good. I'm so glad. Why do you suppose you do it?

JOHN: *(Moving around the room)* Because there's a hell of a lot of horseshit around, and I think I've known it from the beginning.

NINA: Would you care to cite chapter and verse?

JOHN: Sure. Horseshit begins at home.

NINA: He's a wonderful man.

JOHN: He's a hypocrite, kiddo! He's a fake!

NINA: Sssh!

JOHN: Talk about civilization. All that jazz about manners and class and social obligation. He's a poor boy who married a rich girl and doesn't want to be called on it.

NINA: That is a lie! He was only poor after his father died!

JOHN: *(With increasing passion)* Yes, well, all that crap about hard work and nose to the grindstone and burning the midnight oil. What is all that crap? Have you ever seen it in operation? Whenever I tried to call him at the office, he was out playing golf. Have you ever *seen* him *work*? Has he ever brought any work *home*? Have you ever heard him even talk on the *telephone* about work? Have you ever seen him spade the garden or rake a leaf or change a light bulb? I remember one time when I wrote that paper defending the New Deal, he gave me a long lecture about how nobody wants to work in this country, and all the while he was practicing his putting on the back lawn!

NINA: He's done extremely well in business. He sent us to private schools and first-rate colleges.

JOHN: Oh, I know he's done well—on charm, affability, and Mother's money—and a little help from his friends. His friends have carried him all his life. They're the ones who have thrown the deals his way. You ask him a financial question, he'll say, "Wait a minute, I'll call Bill or Bob or Ted."

NINA: Because that's *life*, John! That's what business *is*! The golf course, the backgammon table at the Mid-Day Club, the Saturn Club grill at six—that's where he *works*, you jerk!

JOHN: Well then that's where his family is, not here! Did he ever show you how to throw a ball or dive into a pool? Not him. Mother did all that, while he was off chumming it up with his pals. All he ever taught me was how to hold a fork or answer an invitation or cut in on a pretty girl. He's never been my father and I've never been his son, and he and I have known that for a long time.
(*Pause.* HE *sits exhaustedly on the piano bench.*)

NINA: Well, he's been a wonderful father to me.

JOHN: Maybe so. And maybe to Jigger. I guess that's why I've teased both of you all my life. And why I tease everybody else, for that matter. I'm jealous. I'm jealous of anyone who seems to have a leg up on life, anyone who seems to have a father in the background helping thcm out. Hell, I even tease my own children. I've bent over backwards to be to them what my father never was to me, and then out of some deep-grained jealousy that they have it too good, I tease the pants off them.

NINA: Jesus, John, you're a mess.

JOHN: I know. But I'd be more of one if I didn't write about it.

NINA: Well, write as much as you want, but don't go public on this one.

JOHN: I've already said I won't.

NINA: I'm not sure I believe you, John. You're too angry. You'll change a few words, a few names, and out it will come.

JOHN: Nina, I promise . . .

NINA: Then how come that check is still there? Mother told me about the check, and there it is. How come?

JOHN: I don't want it.

NINA: *(Brings it to him)* Take it, John. Take it, just so I'll be sure. I know you're gentleman enough not to do it if you take the dough.

JOHN: I'll never cash it.
(HE *takes the check.)*

NINA: I don't care, but it's yours now, and the play stays in your desk drawer now, until they're both dead. And until *I'm* dead, goddamnit.

JOHN: *(Putting the check in his wallet)* Or until he changes his mind.

NINA: Fair enough.
(SHE *returns to the couch for more food.)*

JOHN: *(Putting his wallet away)* Actually I'm kind of glad it's not going on, Nina.

NINA: Why?

JOHN: Because, to tell you the truth, I haven't got the plot right yet.

NINA: What's wrong with it?

JOHN: I dunno. It's not right yet. It's not true yet. There's a secret in it somewhere, and I haven't quite nailed it down.

NINA: What secret?

JOHN: Oh, simply the secret of what went wrong between my father and me. Where, when, why did he turn his countenance from me? There must have been a point. Did I wake him too early in the morning with my infant wails before one of those constantly replaceable nurses jammed a bottle in my mouth? Or rather *refused* to jam a bottle in my mouth because I wasn't crying on schedule?

NINA: Here we go . . .

JOHN: Or when I was displayed to family and friend, did I embarrass him by playing with my pee-pee?

NINA: John, you have an absolute obsession with your own penis.

JOHN: Oh—*I* know! Maybe this is what I did: I made the unpardonable mistake of contradicting him—of looking something *up* in the *Book of Knowledge*, and proving him wrong—no, not wrong, that makes no difference, right or wrong—what I did was destroy the "rhythm of the conversation," maybe that's what I did wrong!

NINA: Oh good Lord . . .

JOHN: Yes well, I'd love to know what I did to have him say to himself—and to *me*!—"I don't know this boy. This is not my son." Because he's said it as long as I can remember.

NINA: And if he ever told you he loved you, you'd immediately do some totally irritating thing to make him deny it.

JOHN: You think so?

NINA: I know so. If he killed the fatted calf, you'd complain about the cholesterol.

JOHN: Jesus, Nina.

NINA: You would. I've got your number, John, even if you don't have mine. For instance, I know why you're writing this goddamn play.

JOHN: Why?

NINA: *(Hurriedly, as* SHE *puts on her shoes)* You're writing it because he's dying. You're writing it because you love him. You're writing it to hold onto him after he's gone.
*(*ANN *comes in.)*

ANN: John, don't you want to speak to your brother before your father hangs up?

JOHN: Sure.
*(*HE *grabs some carrots and goes Off upstairs.)*

ANN: *(Distractedly)* Well, that's that.

NINA: What?

ANN: *(Vaguely)* I'd like a splash more, please, Nina.

NINA: *(Getting* ANN'*s glass, going to the bar)* All right.

ANN: Just a splash. I'm serious.

NINA: All right.

ANN: *(Sinking onto the couch)* I give up.

NINA: What's the *trouble*, Mother?

ANN: Jigger. Jigger's the trouble. He wants to move to California.

NINA: What?

ANN: He wants to pick up stakes and move. Wife, children, off they go.

NINA: What's in California?

ANN: A job. A new job. There's a man out there who builds wooden boats, who wants Jigger to work for him. For *half* of what he's making now.

NINA: But why?

ANN: Because he wants to. He says it's something he's always wanted to do.

NINA: He's always liked boats.

ANN: Don't I know it. That canoe he built in the basement. Those sailboats out on the lake . . .

NINA: *(Joining her on the couch)* Which had to be *wood*, remember? No fiberglass allowed. All that labor every spring, because only wood sat naturally on the water . . .

ANN: Between his boats and your dogs we hardly had time to think around here.

NINA: He felt free on the water. I wish *I* felt free about something.

ANN: Well I hear they feel free about *every*thing in California.

NINA: And he's just . . . going?

ANN: Says he is. Says he plans to buy one of those grubby vans, and lug everyone out, like a bunch of Okies. Your father is frantically trying to talk him out of it.

NINA: *(Musingly)* I should just go to Cleveland to that dog school.

ANN: Oh, Nina. Think of Ed.

NINA: I *have* thought of Ed. We've talked about it. He says, do it. Which makes it all the harder.

ANN: I should hope so.

NINA: Still. Maybe I should. I should just do it. What would you say if I did it, Mother?

ANN: Go to *Cleve*land?

NINA: Three days a week.

ANN: Just to be with *dogs*?

NINA: To *work* with them, Mother.

ANN: I've never understood your fascination with dogs.

NINA: I don't know. When I'm with them, I feel I'm in touch with something . . . basic.

ANN: Horses I can understand. The thrill of riding. The excitement of the hunt. The men.

NINA: The men?

ANN: There used to be a lot of attractive men around stables.

NINA: Mother!

ANN: Just as there are around garages today.

NINA: Are you serious?

ANN: But I don't think they hang around kennels.

NINA: I'm interested in *dogs*, Mother.

ANN: I know you are, darling, and I don't think that's any reason to change your life. I mean if you had met some man . . .

NINA: Mother, have you ever watched any of those Nature things on TV?

ANN: I love them. Every Sunday night . . .

NINA: I mean, you see animals, birds, even insects operating under these incredibly complicated instincts. Courting, building their nests, rearing their young in the most amazing complex way . . .

ANN: Amazing behavior . . .

NINA: Well, I think people have these instincts, too.

ANN: Well, I'm sure we do, darling, but . . .

NINA: No, but I mean many more than we realize. I think they're built into our blood, and I think we're most alive when we feel them happening to us.

ANN: Oh well now, I don't know . . .

NINA: I feel most alive when I'm with animals, Mother. Really. I feel some instinctive connection. Put me with a dog, cat, anything, and I feel I'm in touch with a whole different dimension . . . It's as if both of us . . . me and the animal . . . were reaching back across hundreds of thousands of years to a place where we both knew each other much better. There's something there, Mother. I know there's something there.

ANN: On Nina, you sound like one of those peculiar women who wander around Africa falling in love with gorillas.

NINA: Maybe I do. *(Pause)* I hope I do. *(Pause)* I'd rather sound like that than just an echo of you, Mother.

ANN: Well. I think we're all getting too wound up over boats and dogs. People, yes. Boats and dogs, no. The whole family seems to be suddenly going to pieces over boats and dogs.

NINA: And plays, Mother.

ANN: Yes. All right. And plays.
(BRADLEY comes in from upstairs.)

BRADLEY: We've lost him.

ANN: Oh now, darling.

BRADLEY: We've lost him.

ANN: Oh no.

BRADLEY: I'll never see him again.

ANN: Oh, darling.

BRADLEY: I'll be lucky if he comes to my funeral.

ANN: Now, now. I'll tell you one thing. A good *meal* will make us all feel much better.

NINA: I'll tell Shirley.

BRADLEY: Her name is Sharon.

ANN: I still think it's Cheryl.

NINA: Well, whatever it is, I'll tell her we're ready to *eat*! (SHE *goes out.* BRADLEY *goes to the bar.)*

ANN: I wouldn't drink any more, sweetie. We're about to eat.

BRADLEY: I need this.

ANN: How about some wine with dinner? We'll have that.

BRADLEY: Wine won't do it.

ANN: Oh, Bradley . . .

BRADLEY: *(Moving around the room)* I've lost my son. My son is moving three thousand miles away. I'm too old and sick and tired to go see him. And he'll be too tied up in his work to come see me.

ANN: *(Following him)* Oh now, sweetheart . . .

BRADLEY: There are men, there are men in this world whose sons stay with them all the days of their lives. Fred Tillinghast's sons *work* with him every day at the office. He has lunch with them at noon, he has cocktails with them at night, he plays golf with them on weekends. They discuss everything together. Money, women, they're always completely at ease. When he went to Europe, those boys went with him and carried his bags. What did he do to deserve such luck? What did he do that I didn't? I've given my sons everything. I gave them an allowance every week of their lives. I gave them stock. I gave them the maximum deductible gift every Christmas. And now what happens? I reach my final years, my final moments, the nadir of my life, and one son attacks me

while the other deserts me. Oh, it is not to be borne, my love. It is not to be borne.
(HE *sinks into his chair.*)

ANN: Oh, now just wait, Bradley. Maybe John is talking him out of it.

BRADLEY: John?

ANN: John always had a big influence on him.

BRADLEY: John? Jigger and John have fought all their lives. *I'm* the influence. I'm the father. What can John possibly say that I haven't said?
(JOHN *enters quickly.*)

JOHN: I told him he should go.

BRADLEY: You didn't.

ANN: John!

JOHN: Sure. I said, go on. Make your move!! How many guys in the world get a chance to do what they really want?

BRADLEY: I should never have let you near that telephone.

ANN: I'm not sure that was entirely helpful, John.

BRADLEY: He has a fine job where he is.

JOHN: Pushing papers around a desk. Dealing with clients all weekend.

BRADLEY: That's an excellent job. He has a decent salary. He's made all sorts of friends. I got him that job through Phil Foster.

JOHN: You might as well know something else. Pop. I got him this new one.

BRADLEY: You?

JOHN: I put him on to it. The boatyard is owned by a college classmate of mine. I read about it in the *Alumni Review* and got an interview for Jigger.

BRADLEY: Why?

JOHN: Because he was miserable where he was.

BRADLEY: I should have known you were behind all this . . .

JOHN: He hated that job, Pop. Now he can work with boats, and join the Sierra Club, and do all that stuff he loves to do.

BRADLEY: It was none of your damn business.

JOHN: He's my brother!

BRADLEY: I'm his father! Me!
(NINA *enters.)*

JOHN: Well, I'm glad he's going, Pop. And I think Nina should work in Cleveland, too . . . I think you you should, Nina.

NINA: I think I will.

ANN: Oh Nina, no!

BRADLEY: That's ridiculous.

JOHN: So what if Ed has to cook his own spaghetti occasionally . . .

NINA: He'd do it gladly.

BRADLEY: Nonsense. Ed can't cook spaghetti . . .

NINA: No. I think I'll do it. I think I'll go. I'll stay there, and study there, and come home when I can. Put that in your play and write it, John.

JOHN: Maybe I will.

NINA: Sure. Have the goddess Diana come downstage and plant her feet, and give this marvelous speech about seeing-eye dogs, which will bring the audience rising to its feet, and cause your friends the critics to systematically pee in their pants!

ANN: That's not attractive, Nina.

JOHN: I don't know. I kind of liked it.

BRADLEY: You kind of like playing God around here, don't you?

ANN: Yes, John, I really think you should stop managing other people's lives.

BRADLEY: Yes. Do that in your plays if you have to, not in real life.

JOHN: Oh yeah? Well, I'm glad we're talking about real life now, Pop. Because that's something we could use a little more *of*, around here. Hey. Know what? The cocktail hour is over, Pop. It's dead. It's gone. I think Jigger sensed it thirty years ago, and now Nina knows it too, and they're both *trying* to put something back into the world after all these years of a free ride.

BRADLEY: And you? What are you putting back into the world?

JOHN: Me?

BRADLEY: You.

JOHN: I'm writing about it. At least I have the balls to do that.

BRADLEY: Leave this room!

ANN: Oh Bradley . . .

JOHN: Maybe I should leave altogether.

BRADLEY: Maybe you should.

NINA: Oh Pop . . .

JOHN: *(Grabbing his bag in the hall)* Lucky I didn't unpack . . .

ANN: John, now stop . . .

JOHN: *(Throwing on his raincoat)* Call Ellen, Nina. Tell her I'm coming home. Say I'm being banished because of my balls!

BRADLEY: I will not allow you to speak vulgarities in this house!

JOHN: Balls? Balls are vulgar?

ANN: Now that's enough.

JOHN: *(Coming back into the room)* Does that mean that you don't have any, Pop? Does that mean we should all just sit on our ass and watch the world go by?

ANN: *(Going to front hall)* I think it's time to eat.

BRADLEY: I'll tell you what it means. It means that vulgar people always fall back on vulgar language.

ANN: *(Beckoning to* NINA*)* What's the food situation, Nina?

BRADLEY: It means that there are more important things in the world than bodily references.

ANN: *(At the doorway)* Food! Yoo-hoo, everybody! Food!

BRADLEY: It means that your mother and I, and your grandparents on both sides, and Aunt Jane and Uncle Roger and Cousin Esther, and your forebears who came to this country in the seventeenth *century* have all spent their lives trying to establish something called civilization in this wilderness, and so long as I am alive, I will not allow foul-minded and resentful people to tear it all down.
(HE *storms Off and upstairs. Long pause.)*

ANN: Well. You were right about one thing, John: the cocktail hour is definitely over.

NINA: Um. Not quite, Mother.

ANN: What do you mean?

NINA: Come sit down, Mother.

ANN: Don't tell me there is more bad news from the kitchen.

NINA: *(Going to her)* The roast beef is a little the worse for wear.

ANN: What?

NINA: The roast is ruined.

ANN: No.

NINA: Sheila got confused.

ANN: Sheila?

NINA: It's Sheila Marie. I know, because I just made out her check and said she could go.

ANN: What did she do?

NINA: She thought the microwave thing was a warming oven. It came out looking like a shrunken head.

ANN: Oh, I can't *stand* it!

NINA: The peas are still good, and I found some perfectly adequate lamb chops in the freezer. They won't take too long.

ANN: Thank you, darling. Would you tell your father? I imagine he's upstairs in the television room, cooling off on the hockey game.

NINA: *(Taking one of the hors d'oeuvres plates)* I'll take him up some cheese, just to hold him.
(SHE *goes Off and upstairs.)*

ANN: *(Calling after her)* You're a peach, Nina. You really are. Those dogs don't deserve you. *(Pause)* That was an absolutely lovely rib roast of beef.

JOHN: I'm sure.

ANN: Twenty-eight dollars. At the Ex-Cell.

JOHN: I can believe it.

ANN: I suppose Portia might like it. Nina can give it to Portia.

JOHN: Good idea.
(Pause)

ANN: *(Beginning to clean up)* I don't know why I'm talking to you, John. I'm very angry. You've caused nothing but trouble since the minute you arrived.

JOHN: Story of my life.

ANN: I'm afraid it is.

JOHN: I wish I knew why.

ANN: Isn't that what your psychiatrist is supposed to explain, at one hundred dollars a throw?

JOHN: He never could.

ANN: Then I was right: They're a waste of money.
(SHE *starts out.*)
I'd better check on those lamb chops.

JOHN: Mother . . .
(SHE *stops.*)
Since I've been here, I've discovered a big problem with this play of mine.

ANN: I'd say it had lots of problems. In my humble opinion.

JOHN: Well. I've discovered a big problem. It's missing an obligatory scene.

ANN: And what in heaven's name is that?

JOHN: It's a scene which sooner or later has to happen. It's an essential scene. Without it, everyone walks out feeling discontent and frustrated.

ANN: I suppose you mean some ghastly confrontation with your father.

JOHN: Hell no. I've got plenty of those.

ANN: You've got too many of those.

JOHN: I'm thinking of a scene with you, Mother.

ANN: With me?

JOHN: That's what's been missing all my life, Mother.

ANN: Oh, John, please don't get melodramatic.
(SHE *starts out again.*)

JOHN: I've also discovered why it's been missing.
ANN: Why?

JOHN: Because you don't want it to happen.

ANN: I'll tell you what I want to have happen, John. I want us all to sit down together and have a pleasant meal. That's all I want to have happen at the moment, thank you very much.

JOHN: *(Leading her to the couch)* Oh come on, Mother. Please. This is the ideal moment. Pop's sulking upstairs. Nina's busy in the kitchen. And you and I are both a little smashed, which will make it easier. Tell me just one thing.

ANN: What thing?

JOHN: What went wrong when I was very young. Something went wrong. There was some short circuit . . . some problem . . . something . . . What was it?

ANN: I don't know what you're talking about.

JOHN: Come on, Mother. Please. Think back.

ANN: *(Getting up)* John, I am not going to sit around and rake over a lot of old coals. Life's too short and I'm too old, and thank you very much.
(SHE *goes out to the kitchen*)

JOHN: *(Calling after her)* And once again, there goes the obligatory scene, right out the door!
(A moment. Then ANN *comes back in, putting on an apron.)*

ANN: You got lost in the shuffle, John. That's what went wrong. I mean, there you were, born in the heart of the Depression, your father frantic about money, nurses and maids leaving every other day—nobody paid much attention to you, I'm afraid. When Nina was born, we were all dancing around thinking we were the Great Gatsby, and when Jigger came along, we began to settle down. But you, poor soul, were caught in the middle. You lay in your crib screaming for attention, and I'm afraid you've been doing it ever since.

JOHN: That's it?

ANN: That's it. In a nutshell. Now I feel very badly about it, John. I always have. That's why I've found it hard to talk about. I've worked hard to make it up, I promise, but sometimes, no matter how hard you work, you just can't hammer out all the dents.
(SHE *turns to leave again.*)

JOHN: Exit my mother, after a brief, unsatisfactory exchange . . .

ANN: That's right. Because your mother is now responsible for a meal.

JOHN: *(Blocking her way)* I can see the scene going on just a tad longer, Mother.

ANN: How?

JOHN: I think there's more to be said.

ANN: About what?

JOHN: About you, Mother.

ANN: Me?

JOHN: You. I think there's much more to be said about you.

ANN: Such as?

JOHN: Such as, where were you, while the king was in the counting house and the kid was in his cradle?

ANN: I was . . . here, of course.

JOHN: Didn't you pick me up, if I was screaming in my crib?

ANN: Yes. Sometimes. Yes.

JOHN: But not enough?

ANN: No. Not enough.

JOHN: Why not?
(Pause)

ANN: Because . . . because at that point I was a little preoccupied.

JOHN: With what?

ANN: Oh, John.

JOHN: With what?

ANN: I don't have to say.

JOHN: With *what*, Mother?
(Pause)

ANN: I was writing a book.

JOHN: You were what?

ANN: I was sitting right at that desk, all day, every day, writing a big, long book. It took too much of my time, and too much of my thoughts, and I'm sorry if it made me neglect you . . . I've never told anyone about that book.

JOHN: Doesn't it feel good to tell me?

ANN: Not particularly. No.
(SHE *sits at the desk.)*

JOHN: What happened to it?

ANN: I burned it.

JOHN: You burned it?

ANN: All six hundred and twenty-two pages of it. Right in that fireplace. One day, while your father was playing golf.

JOHN: Why?

ANN: Because I didn't like it. I couldn't get it right. It was wrong.

JOHN: Wow, Mother!

ANN: I know it. *(Pause)* But then we had Jigger, and that took my mind off it.

JOHN: What was the book about, Mother?

ANN: I won't tell.

JOHN: Oh, come on.

ANN: I've never told a soul.

JOHN: One writer to another, Mother.

ANN: Never.

JOHN: You mean, the book you wrote instead of nursing me, the book that took my place at your breast . . .

ANN: Oh, John, really.

JOHN: The six-hundred-page book that preoccupied your mind during a crucial formative period of my own, I'll never get to know about. Boy. Talk about hammering out dents, Mother. You've just bashed in my entire front end.
(Pause)

ANN: I'll give you a brief summary of the plot.

JOHN: O.K.

ANN: Brief. You'll have to fill things in as best you can.

JOHN: O.K.
(HE *quickly gets a chair from the hall, and straddles it, next to her.)*

ANN: *(Taken aback)* First, though, I will have a splash more.

JOHN: Sure.

ANN: Just a splash. I'm serious.

JOHN: All right, Mother.
(HE hurriedly mixes her martini.)

ANN: I mean, it's no easy thing to tell one's own son one's innermost thoughts. Particularly when that son tends to be slightly critical.

JOHN: I won't criticize, Mother. I swear.
(HE brings her her drink and again straddles the chair beside her.)

ANN: *(After taking a sip)* All right, then. My book was about a woman.

JOHN: A woman.

ANN: A governess.

JOHN: A governess?

ANN: A well-born woman who goes to work for a distinguished man and supervises the upbringing of his children.

JOHN: Sounds like *Jane Eyre.*

ANN: If you make any cracks, I won't tell you any more.

JOHN: Sorry, Mother. It sounds good.

ANN: Now, this woman, this governess, does *not* fall in love with her employer. Unlike Jane Eyre.

JOHN: She does not?

ANN: No. She falls in love with someone else.

JOHN: Someone else.

ANN: She falls in love with a groom.

JOHN: A groom?

ANN: A very attractive groom. At the stable. Where she keeps her horse.

JOHN: I'm with you, Mother.

ANN: She has a brief, tempestuous affair with the man who saddles her horse.

JOHN: I see.

ANN: Well, it doesn't work out, so she terminates the affair. But the groom gets so upset, he sets fire to the stable.

JOHN: Sets fire.

ANN: The fire symbolizes his tempestuous passion.

JOHN: I see.

ANN: Naturally, she rushes into the flames to save the horses. And she gets thoroughly burned. All over her face. It's horrible.

JOHN: She is punished, in other words, for her indiscretion.

ANN: Yes. That's right. That's it exactly. But finally her wounds heal. The doctor arrives to take off the bandages. Everyone stands around to see. And guess what? She is perfectly beautiful. She is even more beautiful than she was before. The children cluster around her, the master of the house embraces her, and so she marries this man who has loved her all along. You see? Her experience has helped her. In the long run. *(Pause)* Anyway, that's the end. *(Pause)* You can see why I burned it. *(Pause)* You can see why I haven't told anyone about it, all these years. *(Pause)* It's terribly corny, isn't it?

JOHN: No, Mother.

ANN: It's silly.

JOHN: No, it says a lot.
(HE *kisses her on the cheek.)*

ANN: John, you're embarrassing me.

JOHN: No, really. It's very touching.

ANN: Well, I never could get the *feelings* right. Especially with that groom. That passion. That tempestuous passion. Those . . . flames. I could never get that right in my book.

JOHN: I never could either, in a play.

ANN: Oh, it would be impossible in a play.

JOHN: Maybe.

ANN: That's why I wish you would write a good, long, wonderful book.
(SHE *gets up*)
And now I really ought to give Nina a hand with supper.

JOHN: Mother, one more question . . .

ANN: You've asked too many.

JOHN: About the groom.

ANN: Ah, the groom.

JOHN: What happened to him?

ANN: Oh heavens. I can't remember. I think I sent him off to Venezuela or somewhere.

JOHN: In the book?

ANN: In the book.

JOHN: But what happened in life, Mother.

ANN: In *life*?

JOHN: Where did he go? Who was he?

ANN: I never said he *existed*, John. This . . . groom.

JOHN: But he did, didn't he? You met him before you had me. And he left after I was born. And you sat down and wrote about him. Now come on. Who was he?

ANN: John . . .

JOHN: Please, Mother. Tell me.

ANN: It was over forty years ago . . .

JOHN: Still, Mother. Come on. Whom did you base him on?

ANN: Oh, John, I don't know . . . Maybe I'm getting old
. . . or maybe I've had too many cocktails . . . but I'm
beginning to think I based him on your father.
(SHE *starts out as* BRADLEY *comes in.*)

BRADLEY: Based what on me?

ANN: My life, darling. I've based my life on you.
(SHE *kisses him and goes out. Pause.*)

BRADLEY: Your mother always knows when to walk out of
a room.

JOHN: My mother is full of surprises.

BRADLEY: Well, she instinctively senses when a man needs
to do business with another man. And out she goes.

JOHN: We're going to do business, Pop?

BRADLEY: *(Going to his chair)* We're going to talk seriously. And I hope when you have to talk seriously with
one of your sons, your sweet Ellen will bow out just as
gracefully.

JOHN: What's on your mind, Pop?

BRADLEY: First, I'd like a glass of soda water, please.

JOHN: I'll have one, too.

BRADLEY: Good. Time for sermons and soda water, eh?

JOHN: It sure does feel like the day after.
(JOHN *fixes the two drinks.*)

BRADLEY: John: you and I spoke angry words to each other
a while back. It was most unfortunate. I blame you, I
blame myself, and I blame alcohol. There's nothing more
dangerous than a lengthy cocktail hour.

JOHN: I apologize, Pop. I got carried away.

BRADLEY: We both got carried away. We screamed and shouted, didn't we? Well, at least we didn't take off our clothes.

JOHN: Here's your soda water, Pop.

BRADLEY: Thank you, John. You know what I did upstairs instead of watching the hockey?

JOHN: What?

BRADLEY: I sat and thought. I thought about all of you. I thought about . . . my father. Do you suppose all families are doomed to disperse?

JOHN: Most of them do, Pop. Eventually. In this country.

BRADLEY: You don't think it's . . . me?

JOHN: No, Pop.

BRADLEY: People seem to want to leave me. There seems to be this centrifugal force.

JOHN: That's life, Pop.

BRADLEY: Well, whatever it is, I can't fight it any more . . . When I was upstairs, I telephoned Jigger. I called him back.

JOHN: Oh yes?

BRADLEY: What is it Horace Greeley tells us? "Go west, young man"? Well, he's young. It's there. I gave him my blessing.

JOHN: *(Sitting near him)* That's good, Pop.

BRADLEY: "The old oak must bend with the wind . . . or break . . ." *(Looks at* JOHN) Isn't that from Virgil?

JOHN: I think it's T. S. Eliot.
*(*BOTH *laugh.)*
But don't look it up.
*(*THEY *laugh again.)*

BRADLEY: Maybe I've loved him too much. Maybe I've loved him at your expense. Do you think that's true? *(Pause)*

JOHN: *(Carefully)* I don't know . . .

BRADLEY: Maybe he's trying to get away from me. What do you think?

JOHN: I think . . . *(Pause)* I think maybe he's trying to get away from all of us. I think maybe I got him to go because I was jealous. Hell, I think we all put our own spin on the ball—you, me, Nina, Mother—and guess what: it no longer matters. Jigger likes *boats*, Pop. He likes working with *wood*. Maybe he'll build a new clipper ship.

BRADLEY: Well, the point is, he'll be happy there. Sailing. He's a magnificent sailor. Remember right here on Lake Erie?

JOHN: I remember . . .

BRADLEY: I could sit in my office and look out on the lake, and sometimes I think I could actually see his sails . . .

JOHN: Yes . . .

BRADLEY: Of course, that friend of yours is hardly paying him a nickel out there. Hardly a plug nickel. And they'll have to buy a house. I mean, they all can't live in that stupid van. Even after he sells his house here, he'll need a considerable amount of additional cash. So I told him I'd send him a check.
(BRADLEY begins to look at, around, and under the table next to him for the check HE gave to JOHN.)
And I told him the cupboard was a little bare, at the moment. A little bare. I'm no longer collecting a salary, as you know, and I do need to keep a little cash on hand these days. Doctors . . . Pills . . . If I should have to go into the hospital . . .
(JOHN takes the check out of his wallet, hands it to BRADLEY)

JOHN: Here you go, Pop.

BRADLEY: *(Taking it)* Thank you, John. *(Pause)* I mean, I refuse to sell stock. I can't do that. When I die, I want your mother to have . . . I want all of you to have . . . I've got to leave something.

JOHN: I know, Pop.
*(*NINA *comes on.)*

NINA: I think we're almost ready to eat. Just so you'll know.
*(*SHE *takes the hors d'oeuvres plate, starts out.)*

JOHN: We're discussing the National Debt.

NINA: Oh.
(Then SHE *stops.)*
Come to think of it, Pop, you could do me one hell of a big favor.

BRADLEY: What, Pookins?

NINA: *(Going to him)* I wonder if I could ask for a little money.

BRADLEY: Money?

NINA: *(Sitting on the arm of his chair)* For Cleveland. Tuition. Travel. Living expenses. It costs money to change your life.

BRADLEY: I'm sure that Ed . . .

NINA: Ed would subsidize my commuting to the moon, if I asked him. Which is why I won't. I want to get back on the gravy train for a while, Pop. I'll borrow from you and pay you back, once I have a job. It's as simple as that.

BRADLEY: We'll work out something, Pookins. I promise.

NINA: Oh thanks, Pop. I knew you would.
(Kisses him, and starts to exit gloatingly.)
And as for you, John, I think you should go get yourself

a good dog. I'll tell you why but first I have to toss the salad.

(SHE *goes off.*)

BRADLEY: I suppose she'll want at least twenty as well.

JOHN: She might.

BRADLEY: And she should get it. It's only fair.

JOHN: Right.

BRADLEY: I am *not* going to cut into capital.

JOHN: I know . . .

BRADLEY: My father used to tell me every moment of his life . . .

JOHN: I know . . .

BRADLEY: Even as it is, I'm cutting close to the bone . . .

JOHN: You'll live, Pop.

BRADLEY: No, I won't. I'll die. But I'll die fair. I'll add twenty extra for you in my will. That's a promise. I'll call Bill Sawyer first thing.

JOHN: Thanks, Pop.

BRADLEY: So: you all get exactly the same amount of money.

JOHN: That's right.

BRADLEY: Jigger gets his boats . . . Nina gets her dogs . . .

JOHN: Right, Pop . . .

BRADLEY: And all I have to worry about is that damn play.

JOHN: It's not going on, Pop.

BRADLEY: *(Getting up)* If only you'd put in some of the good things. The singing around the piano, for example. That was good. Or the skiing. That was very good. That's when we were at our best.

JOHN: It's hard to put skiing on the stage, Pop.

BRADLEY: You could talk about it. You could at least mention it.

JOHN: I do, actually. I bring it up.

BRADLEY: You do? You mention the skiing?

JOHN: The skiing and the piano both.

BRADLEY: Do you think you could mention anything else? (ANN'S VOICE *is heard from Offstage.*)

ANN'S VOICE: I'm about to light the candles!

BRADLEY: (*Calling off*) Two more minutes, darling! Just two! (*To* JOHN) I mean, if I were writing the darned thing, I'd want to prove to those critics we *are* worth writing about. I'd put our best foot forward, up and down the line.

JOHN: I have to call 'em as I see 'em, Pop.

BRADLEY: That's what I'm afraid of.
(ANN *appears at the door.*)

ANN: Now Nina has just whipped together a perfectly spectacular meal. There's even mint sauce to go with the lamb chops. Now come on, or it will all get cold.

BRADLEY: Just a minute more, my love. We're discussing the future of American drama.

ANN: Couldn't you discuss it in the dining room?

BRADLEY: I'm not sure I can.

ANN: Well hurry, or Nina and I will sit down and dig in all by ourselves.
(SHE *goes off.* JOHN *takes a necktie out of his jacket pocket, and begins to put it on, looking in a wall mirror.*)

BRADLEY: What happens at the end of this play? Do you have me die?

JOHN: No, Pop.

BRADLEY: Sure you don't kill me off?

JOHN: Promise.

BRADLEY: Then how do you leave me in the end?

JOHN: I'm not sure now.

BRADLEY: You could mention my charities, for example. You could say I've tried to be very generous.

JOHN: I could . . .

BRADLEY: Or you could refer to my feelings for your mother. You should say I've adored her for almost fifty years.

JOHN: I'll think about it, Pop . . .
(NINA *enters.*)

NINA: Those lamb chops are just lying there, looking at us!
(NINA *exits.* ANN's *laughter is heard Offstage.*)

BRADLEY: I suppose what you need is a kicker at the end of your play.

JOHN: A kicker?

BRADLEY: When I give a speech, I try to end with a kicker.

JOHN: A kicker.

BRADLEY: Some final point which pulls everything together.

JOHN: In the theater, they call that a button.

BRADLEY: Well, whatever it is, it makes people applaud.

JOHN: You can't *make* people applaud, Pop . . .

BRADLEY: You can generate an appreciative mood. I mean, isn't that what we want, really? Both of us? In the end? Isn't that why I make speeches and you write plays? Isn't that why people go to the theater? Don't we all want to celebrate something at the end of the day?

JOHN: I guess we do.

BRADLEY: Of course we do. In spite of all our difficulties, surely we can agree on that. So find a good kicker for the end.

JOHN: Kicker, kicker, who's got the kicker?

BRADLEY: *(Picking up the script gingerly, like a dead fish, and handing it to him)* Meanwhile, here. Put this away somewhere, so it doesn't dominate the rest of our lives.

JOHN: *(Taking it)* O.K., Pop.

BRADLEY: *(Turning off various lights)* Because there are other things in the world besides plays . . .

JOHN: Pop . . .

BRADLEY: Good food . . . congenial conversation . . . the company of lovely women . . .

JOHN: I've just thought of a kicker, Pop.

BRADLEY: Now *please* don't settle for some smart remark.

JOHN: Pop, listen. Remember the plot I was telling you about? Where the older son thinks he's illegitimate?

BRADLEY: *(Starting out)* I can't discuss it.

JOHN: No, no, Pop. Wait. Please. Here's the thing: suppose, in the end, he discovers he's the true son of his father, after all.
(BRADLEY stops, turns, looks at him.)

BRADLEY: That just might do it.
(ANN comes in again.)

ANN: Now come ON. Nothing can be more important than a good meal. Bring the tray, please, John, so that we don't have to stare at a lot of old liquor bottles after dinner.
(To BRADLEY, taking his arm) Wait till you see what Nina has produced for dessert . . .

BRADLEY: *(As* HE *goes, over his shoulder, to* JOHN*)* . . . I still don't like your title, John. Why don't you simply call it *The Good Father?* . . .
*(*JOHN *stands, holding his play, watching his* PARENTS *go Off, as the lights fade quickly)*

THE END

ANOTHER ANTIGONE

ANOTHER ANTIGONE was first produced in March, 1987, at The Old Globe Theatre in San Diego, California, with the following cast:

HENRY   George Grizzard
JUDY   Marissa Chibas
DIANA   Debra Mooney
DAVE   Steven Flynn

It was directed by John Tillinger, designed by Steven Rubin, lit by Kent Dorsey. The stage manager was Dianne De Vita.

The play opened at Playwrights Horizons in New York City in January, 1988. The cast, director, and designers remained the same. The stage manager, in this case, was Neal Ann Stephens.

To John Tillinger

CAST OF
CHARACTERS

HENRY HARPER   Professor of Classics
JUDY MILLER   a student
DIANA EBERHART   Dean of Humane Studies
DAVID APPLETON   a student

The play takes place in a university in Boston during the latter half of the spring term.

It is designed, as Sophocles' *Antigone* was, to be performed without an intermission.

The general effect of the set should evoke the Greek Revival architecture of a typical New England college. There should be columns and steps and benches. Somewhere in the center there should be a slightly abstracted desk and two chairs, indicating both Henry's and Diana's office. Near it is a bookcase, a filing cabinet, on which is an old hot plate, a possibly tin coffee pot, and a couple of cracked mugs. The general effect should be multi-scenic, fluid and shifting, indoors and out, and vaguely Greek.

AT RISE: *Henry sits at his desk, perusing a typewritten paper. Judy sits in the other chair. She watches intently. He is middle-aged and conservatively dressed. She, in her early twenties, is casually dressed in whatever students are currently wearing.*

HENRY: *(Finally, putting the document down neatly on the desk between them)* Another Antigone.

JUDY: Did someone else write one?

HENRY: Sophocles wrote one.

JUDY: No, I mean someone in *class*.

HENRY: Aeschylus wrote one, which is lost. Euripides we *think* wrote one. Seneca tried to write one. Voltaire tried not to. Jean Anouilh wrote a rather peculiar one in 1944, during the Nazi occupation of Paris.

JUDY: But I'm the only one in *class* who wrote one.

HENRY: *(Weak smile)* That's right. *(Pause.)* This year.

JUDY: You mean, other students wrote them in other years?

HENRY: Oh yes.

JUDY: Really?

HENRY: Of course. (HENRY *goes to the filing cabinet.* HE *pulls out a drawer.*) Let's see . . . Antigone . . . Antigone . . . (HE *thumbs through a file of old folders and records.*)

Here we are. *Antigone.* (HE *takes out a particular folder.*) Now. I have a record of one in 1955, written during the McCarthy hearings. And another, by a student who I recall was black, about the civil rights movement in 1963. And of course there were two, no, three, which cropped up during the Vietnam war.

JUDY: Did anyone ever deal with the nuclear arms race before?

HENRY: No. As far as I know, you are the first to apply the Antigone myth to that particular topic.

JUDY: The story really turned me on.

HENRY: I'm glad it did. It is one of the great works of Western literature. Antigone herself is the classic rebel, the ancestor to such figures as Saint Joan or Martin Luther.

JUDY: Oh yes. I see that.

HENRY: And Creon is the ultimate image of uncompromising political authority.

JUDY: I got that, too.

HENRY: Their clash is inevitable and tragic.

JUDY: I understand. *(Indicating her manuscript)* I tried to make them like Jane Fonda and Ronald Reagan.

HENRY: I know what you tried to do, Miss . . . uh . . . Miss . . . (HE *glances at her title page.*) Miller. I read all . . . (HE *glances at the last page.*) twelve pages of it, in preparation for this conference.
(HE *slides the script across the desk to her.* SHE *takes it, looks at the title page, flips through it, looks at the last page, then looks at him.*)

JUDY: You didn't mark it.

HENRY: I most certainly did. I underlined several run-on sentences, and I circled a rather startling number of misspelled words.

JUDY: No, I mean you didn't *grade* it.

HENRY: No, I didn't.

JUDY: Why not?

HENRY: Because this course is about Greek tragedy, and your paper isn't.

JUDY: Did you grade those other *Antigone's*?

HENRY: I most certainly did not. I simply keep a record of them on file, the way the Pope keeps a file on various heresies.

JUDY: Well mine isn't a heresy!

HENRY: It is, to me.

JUDY: Don't you believe in nuclear disarmament?

HENRY: Of course I do. I think the arms race is madness.

JUDY: Then don't you think these things should be said?

HENRY: Absolutely. And I believe I said them, back in February, when I was discussing the political background of Greek drama. Then, if you'll remember, I compared Athens and Sparta, and pointed out rather frightening analogies to the United States and the Soviet Union.

JUDY: I had mono in February.

HENRY: Mono?

JUDY: Nucleosis. I kept falling asleep at the Film Festival, even during *Psycho*.

HENRY: I'm sorry to hear that. You must get the notes, then, from a fellow student. You might need them when you write your term paper.

JUDY: But this *is* my term paper.

HENRY: It's not on an assigned topic.

JUDY: It's on *Antigone*.

HENRY: But it's not on Sophocles.

JUDY: But I spent two weeks working on it.

HENRY: Sophocles spent two years.

JUDY: But I'm taking other courses!

HENRY: And Sophocles didn't—I grant you.

JUDY: Yes, but . . .

HENRY: Miss Miller: At the beginning of the semester, I handed out a list of assigned topics. I stated specifically that any departures from these topics should be cleared through me. Now suddenly, long before the term is over, I discover this odd effort, stuffed under my door, with no previous permission whatsoever.

JUDY: I had to try it first. To see if it worked.

HENRY: Well, you did. And it didn't.

JUDY So, what do I do?

HENRY: You read the texts carefully. You attend class religiously. And in the middle of May, you hand in a fifteen-page, coherently organized, typewritten paper, with adequate margins and appropriate footnotes, on the main issues of this course.

JUDY: Couldn't you give me partial credit? For the idea?

HENRY: Miss Miller, how can I? It's misguided. It's wrong. You have taken one of the world's great plays, and reduced it to a juvenile polemic on current events.

JUDY: Juvenile?

HENRY: I'm sorry.

JUDY: Of course that's your opinion.

HENRY: I'm afraid my opinion is the one that counts.

JUDY: But what if I put it on?

HENRY: On?

JUDY: In front of the class—just reading it out loud.

HENRY: Miss Miller: we have only so much time before the end of the term. We have yet to absorb the very difficult concept of Greek tragedy. I doubt if there's time in class to play show-and-tell.

JUDY: Then I'll do it somewhere else.

HENRY: I'd spend my time on a paper.

JUDY: I'll do my play instead. You could come and see.

HENRY: I'm afraid I'd see a great gap in your education, Miss Miller. As well as in my list of grades.

JUDY: You mean I'd fail?

HENRY: You'd receive an incomplete.

JUDY: Which means, since I'm a senior, that I'd fail. I wouldn't graduate, Professor Harper.

HENRY: Which means you'd better not spend these last valuable days of your academic life on amateur theatrics.
(HE *gets up, begins organizing his books and notes.*)
And now I have to teach a class. And I strongly suspect you have to go to one.
(JUDY *gets up, too.*)

JUDY: Professor Harper, I don't want to sound conceited or anything, but you should know that after I graduate, I've been accepted for a special training program in investment banking at Morgan Guaranty Trust in New York City.

HENRY: My congratulations.

JUDY: Well, in my interview, they were particularly impressed by my leadership qualities, my creativity, and my personal sense of commitment. They wrote me that in a letter, Professor Harper.

HENRY: Congratulations again.

JUDY: I also heard, from someone who works there, that I'm only the second Jewish woman to be brought into that program at that level since its inception.

HENRY: I am virtually overwhelmed.

JUDY: Yes, well, I believe in my abilities, Professor Harper. I plan to apply them. I'm going to put this play *on*. I wrote it, and I like it, and I'm committed to what it says. And if it's no good now, I'll work to make it better. And I'll bet, by the end of the term, you'll be able to give me a straight A.

HENRY: *(Turning, as if at the door)* Miss Miller: After such a magnificent display of American optimism and industry, I'm tempted to give you a straight A right now.

JUDY: Thank you.

HENRY: And I believe I would if this were a course on comedy. But alas, it is not. It's a course on tragedy. And you have just demonstrated that you have no conception of tragedy at all! (HE *goes off, with his books and notes.* JUDY *looks at him, and looks at her paper.* SHE *goes off, reading it aloud).*

JUDY:
People of this land, we suffer under a yoke.
*(*SHE *begins to realize a new pertinence.)*
A tyrant rules our city, and unjust laws
Now squelch all forms of perfectly plausible protest . . .
*(*SHE *goes off. As she goes off,* DIANA *comes on to address the audience. She is a harassed, nervous, middle-aged woman, dressed efficiently.* SHE *speaks to the audience as if it were a group of concerned students. She might speak from note cards.)*

DIANA: Good morning . . . I spoke to you as freshmen. I speak to you now as seniors and what we hope will be very generous alumni . . . The topic of today's meeting is "Preparing for the Future." I'll be brief, since I know all of you are waiting to hear from the Placement people about the world beyond these walls. I do want to make a quick comment on our curriculum, however. A number of you have recently complained about the traditional courses which are still required. Why, you ask, with tuitions so high and the search for jobs so increasingly competitive, are you forced to take such impratical courses? You may be sure, by the way, that the recruiting offices at I.B.M. and General Electric are asking the same question: Why must you take these things? After all, they are concerned only with some book, some poem, some old play. "Only some work," as my special favorite Jane Austen once said, "in which the best powers of the mind are displayed, in the best chosen language." Well, there you are. They're the best. And we need no reason beyond that to justify, for example, Professor Harper's course on Greek tragedy. It deals with the best. It exists. It is there. And will remain there, among several other valuable requirements, for what we hope is a very long time. *(SHE glances offstage.)* And now, Alice Zimmerman, from Placement, will talk to you about . . . *(SHE glances at her note card.)* "The Job Market Jungle versus the Graduate School Grind." Those of you who are tardy may now be seated. *(The late members of the audience may be seated here.)* Have a good morning. *(SHE goes off as DAVE comes on from another direction. HE reads aloud from a typewritten script.)*

DAVE:
"No, Antigone, no. Please reconsider.
Do not take on this dangerous enterprise.
The risks are too great, the payoff insignificant."
(JUDY comes on, as if down the steps of the library, carrying a stack of books.)

JUDY: *(Breathlessly)* Look what I got. *(Reads off the titles) The Nuclear Insanity* . . . *A World Beyond War* . . . *Our Debt to the Future* . . .
I'm going to put all this in.

DAVE: You're racking up a lot of time on this thing.

JUDY: Well I want to make it good. Did you read the first scene?

DAVE: *(Reciting by heart)*
"No, Antigone, no. Please reconsider."

JUDY: What do you think? *(Pause)*

DAVE: You're in blank verse.

JUDY: I know that.

DAVE: Every line.
(Accentuates it)
"Do *not* take *on* this *dang'*rous *enterprise.*"

JUDY: I know.

DAVE: How come?

JUDY: *(Accenting it)* I *just* got *into it* and *coul*dn't *stop.*

DAVE: *(Dramatically, as if it were Shakespeare)*
"The risks are too great, the payoff insignificant."

JUDY: Want to do this?

DAVE: Me?

JUDY: Want to?

DAVE: *(Looking at script)* This is a woman's part. This is her sister talking here.

JUDY: I've changed it. I've made it her lover.

DAVE: Get someone from Drama.

JUDY: I already did. Drama people are doing all the other roles. Please, Dave. Do it.

DAVE: *(Melodramatically)*
"No, Antigone, no. Please reconsider."
(Pause) I better not, Judy.

JUDY: I need company.

DAVE: No thanks.

JUDY: I thought you liked Greek stuff.

DAVE: I do.

JUDY: You even talked me into taking the course.

DAVE: I know, I know.

JUDY: You're always borrowing the books . . .

DAVE: Yeah, but I don't have time for anything anymore. I've got a double lab in my major this term. And a brutal schedule in track every weekend. And, as you know, I'm not doing too well in either.

JUDY: You're doing fine. You're just a slow starter. *(Slyly)* Which is part of your charm.

DAVE: All I know is, you get straight A's, you've got a great job waiting for you on the outside, you can afford to fool around with drama. Me? I've only had one interview so far, and I blew it.

JUDY: You didn't *blow* it, Dave. You just overslept.

DAVE: Yeah well, how can we live together next year if I can't nail down a job in New York? I've got to get my grades up, Jude.

JUDY: All right, Dave. That's cool. I'll look for someone else.
(She takes her own copy of her script out of her backpack, looks at it, looks at him.)
Would you at least read it with me?

DAVE: Sure.

JUDY: From the top?

DAVE: Sure. Why not? *(Reading)*
"Hello, Antigone. And what brings you here,
Worried and out of sorts on this spring morning?
You look like you've got something on—
(Turns page)
—your mind."

JUDY: *(Reading)*
"My friend Lysander—"

DAVE: *(Looking at his script)* Lysander? I have "Beloved sister."

JUDY: That's what I changed. I changed it to Lysander.

DAVE: Lysander? That's Shakespeare. It's from *Midsummer Night's Dream.*

JUDY: It's also Greek. I looked it up.

DAVE: But it's primarily—

JUDY: *(Reads, with feeling)*
"My friend Lysander, will you join with me
In picketing and protesting the bomb
At several local military bases
Where nuclear arms are stored? And would you be willing,
O my loyal Lysander—"

DAVE: Lysander. Sounds like a disinfectant.

JUDY: *(Insistently)*
"Would you be willing, O my loyal Lysander
Even to chain yourself to a chain-link fence
Or lie down in the road in front of a gate
And so prevent all types of vehicular access?"

DAVE: I do.

JUDY:
And if the state police or National Guard,
Accompanied by snarling German shepherds,
Attempted to dislodge us from our task,
Would you be willing, my lover and my friend . . .
To go to jail with me, and then remain
At least till our parents post appropriate bail.
(Pause)

DAVE: Who'll you get for Lysander if I don't do it?

JUDY: Oh probably that blond faternity type who lifts weights and played the lead in *Fool for Love.*

DAVE: Mark Shapiro? *(JUDY nods.)* I'll do Lysander.

JUDY: Now don't if you don't want to.

DAVE: So I get another C in another course.

JUDY: Now think positively, Dave.

DAVE: So I mess up another interview.

JUDY: *(Handing him her script)* I'll buy you a new alarm clock. Read from here.

DAVE: *(Looking at it)* This is all new.

JUDY: I rewrote it last night. With you in mind.

DAVE: You knew I'd do it.

JUDY: I hoped you would. (HENRY *reenters his office, settles into a chair to read a book)*

DAVE: *(Kissing her)*
"Antigone . . .
(Then reading)
Much as I've loved you, even since freshman year,
And lived with you since the second semester of sophomore,
Built you a loft for our bed in off-campus housing,
Prepared your pastas, shared your stereo,
Still I have fears about what you've just proposed.
The risks are too great, the payoff insignificant."

JUDY: What do you think?

DAVE: I love it.

JUDY: You do?

DAVE: I love you.

JUDY: *(Taking the script back)* I don't like it.

DAVE: What's the matter?

JUDY: It sounds wrong. I'm going to rewrite it.

DAVE: Again?

JUDY: *(Gathering up her books and bag)* I'll make it better.

DAVE: What if you cut Lysander?

JUDY: Why? You're good. I'm going to build up his part.

DAVE: *(Following her)*
"No, Antigone, no. Please reconsider."
(They go off as DIANA appears in the doorway to HENRY's office.)

DIANA: Henry?

HENRY: Yes? Come in. *(HE sees her and jumps to his feet.)* Ah. Our Dean. Empress of all Humanities, including Remedial Reading.
(HE gives her an elaborately courtly salute and bow.)

DIANA: Knock it off, Henry.

HENRY: You look particularly lovely today, Diana. What is it? New hairdo? New blouse? New something.

DIANA: It's the same old me, Henry.

HENRY: No, no. There's something different. Maybe it's your eyes. They blaze like beacons 'cross The Hellespont.

DIANA: And it's the same old you, Henry. You've been saying things like that for twenty years.

HENRY: And meaning them, Diana.

DIANA: I used to think you meant them. Now I know different.

HENRY: Dear lady . . .

DIANA: Now I know that you just say these things by rote, Henry. You say them to the librarian in the reserve book room, and you say them to the Xerox woman, and you say them to the cashier in the cafeteria. You say them to keep us all at a distance, so you won't have to say anything else. If any of us *did* have a new blouse, you wouldn't notice it at all.

HENRY: Now, Diana . . .

DIANA: Let's change the channel, shall we, Henry? Something's come up.

HENRY: What dark words seek to escape through the gate of thy teeth?

DIANA: Judy Miller.

HENRY: Judy . . . ?

DIANA: Miller. *(Pause)*

HENRY: Ah, Miss Miller. *(French accent)* L'affaire Antigone.

DIANA: You know that's why I'm here, Henry.

HENRY: I swear I didn't. I have a number of students, a number of courses.

DIANA: You teach two courses, Henry. And you have relatively few students in each. Now let's focus, please, on the issue.

HENRY: Administration has made you cruel as Clytemnestra.

DIANA: Henry, *please. (Pause)*

HENRY: All right. Judy Miller.

DIANA: I understand—

HENRY: Would you like some coffee?
(HE crosses to pour her some.)

DIANA: Yes, please—I understand she brought in a rewritten version.

HENRY: She brought in *two* rewritten versions.

DIANA: Well she brought one to me, as well.

HENRY: The first? Or the second?

DIANA: A third.

HENRY: I said I wouldn't read that one.

DIANA: It's not bad, Henry. It's longer, it's getting better. It's now at least a play.

HENRY: It's hopeless.

DIANA: Give her a B for effort.

HENRY: A *B?* I won't give her any grade at all.

DIANA: A student takes your course, becomes inspired by an old play, writes a modern version . . .

HENRY: And demonstrates thereby that she knows nothing about Sophocles, nothing about the Greeks, nothing about tragedy.

DIANA: Henry, she tried.

HENRY: And failed. A B? A B means good. A B means very good. I am not so far lost in the current inflation of grades as to litter the campus with disposable Bs.

DIANA: Oh, Henry . . .

HENRY: I'm sorry. If I gave her a grade for that nonsense, Diana, it would make the whole course meaningless. *(Pause)* It would make *me* meaningless. *(Pause.* DIANA *lights a cigarette.)* Still smoking, I see.

DIANA: Sometimes.

HENRY: Don't.

DIANA: I smoke, Henry, when I find myself caught in the middle of something. Which seems to be the case a good deal lately with this job.

HENRY: Ah hah. Second thoughts from our Dean. You asked for that job, Diana. You agitated for it. All that chatter about the need for more women at the administrative level. Well, now you've sunk to that level and it's leveling you. Come back to the classroom where you belong.

DIANA: Sometimes I wish I could.

HENRY: *(Taking an ashtray out of a desk drawer, holding it out to her)* At least put out that cigarette. Life is tragic enough without your contributing to it.

DIANA: Let me enjoy it, Henry.

HENRY: Your lungs or mine, Diana. *(HE holds out the ashtray.)* Put it out.

DIANA: You win. *(SHE puts it out; he cleans out the ashtray, puts it away.)* Now let me win one.

HENRY: No.

DIANA: How about partial credit?

HENRY: No.

DIANA: She's a senior. She needs to graduate.

HENRY: I'm sorry. *(Pause)*

DIANA: She's putting it on, you know.

HENRY: The play?

DIANA: She's putting it on.

HENRY: Reading it? In some dining hall?

DIANA: Staging it. She asked my permission to use Spingler Auditorium.

HENRY: You said No.

DIANA: I said Yes.

HENRY: You gave her permission?

DIANA: Of course I gave it to her. I had to give it to her. *(Pause)* I wanted to give it to her.

HENRY: Traitor. Or is it, traitress?

DIANA: Well, I'm sorry, Henry. But there seems to be a lot of interest cropping up for this thing. Several of the student antinuclear groups want to sponsor it. Bill Silverstein is writing some incidental music on the Moog synthesizer. And someone over in Art has agreed to do simple neo-classic scenery. They plan to present it on the Friday night before graduation. For parents. And alumni. And friends.

HENRY: Poor Sophocles . . .

DIANA: Oh now.

HENRY: Set to the tune of a Moog synthesizer.

DIANA: Yes well, it should create quite a stir.

HENRY: Quite a stir! That's it, exactly, Diana! Quite a stir! It will stir up a lot of cheap liberal guilt and a lot of fake liberal piety and a lot of easy liberal anger at the poor Creons of this world who are really working on this nuclear thing, and frantically trying to keep the world from blowing itself up!

DIANA: Oh, Henry . . .

HENRY: Do you know what tragedy is, Diana?

DIANA: I think I do, yes.

HENRY: I don't think you do, Diana. I don't think anyone in this happy-ending country really does. Tragedy means the universe is unjust and unfair, Diana. It means we are hedged about by darkness, doom, and death. It means the good, the just, and well-intentioned don't always *win*, Diana. That's what tragedy means. And if we can learn that, if I can teach that, if I can give these bright, beady-eyed students at least a glimmer of that, then perhaps someday we will be able to join hands with our enemies across the water, or our neighbors down below, or the outcasts in our own back*yard*, and create a common community against this darkness. That's what I believe, Diana. And that's what Sophocles believed in 443 B.C. when he wrote *Antigone*. That's what Shakspeare believed when he wrote *King Lear*. Tragedy keeps us honest, keeps us real, keeps us human. All great nations should have a tragic vision, Diana, and we have none. And that is why I cannot endorse what this woman, no, this *girl*, is doing when she puts on her strident little travesty for the passing parade in Spingler Auditorium on graduation weekend. That is not tragedy, Diana. That is just trouble-making. And I cannot give her credit for it. *(Pause.)*

DIANA: May I have the ashtray back, please?

HENRY: No.

DIANA: I want it *back*, Henry. I don't want to tap ashes all over your floor.

HENRY: *(Handing it to her)* Here.
(Gets up) I'll open the door.

DIANA: I'd leave the door closed, Henry. Open the window if you want. This is private. *(She smokes.)*

HENRY: *(Not opening anything)* Private?

DIANA: Have you given any thoughts to your low enrollments, Henry?

HENRY: Thought? Of course I've given thought. In a world of television and Punk Rock, it's a little difficult to maintain—

DIANA: The Provost thinks there might be another reason, Henry.

HENRY: The Provost?

DIANA: He brought it up last fall, when he saw the registration figures.

HENRY: And what does the Provost think?

DIANA: Apparently . . . over the years . . . there've been complaints about you, Henry.

HENRY: Oh I'm sure. That I take attendance. That I take off for misspellings. That I actually *call* on people in class.

DIANA: No, it's something else, Henry. Some students . . . over the years . . . have complained that you're . . . biased.

HENRY: Biased?

DIANA: Prejudiced.

HENRY: *Prejudiced?*

DIANA: Anti-Semitic, Henry. *(Pause)*

HENRY: Say that again.

DIANA: There's been a pattern of complaints.

HENRY: But on what *grounds?*

DIANA: Apparently the administration thinks you make certain remarks in the classroom. Which students pass on. And cause others to stay away. *(Pause)*

HENRY: This is ridiculous.

DIANA: I agree.

HENRY: And outrageous.

DIANA: I think so, too.

HENRY: It's slander! I'm going to see the Provost right now!

DIANA: Hold on, Henry!

HENRY: I mean this is unconscionable. It's like the time five years ago when poor Bob Klein was accused of some late night unpleasantness in the lab by that little temptress in a T-shirt. He had to resign.

DIANA: He resigned because he was *guilty,* Henry.

HENRY: Well I'm not guilty of anti-Semitism. Or do you think I am?

DIANA: I think you . . . make remarks, Henry.

HENRY: Remarks?

DIANA: For example, in the curriculum meeting last fall . . .

HENRY: What did I say?

DIANA: You told that joke.

HENRY: It was a good joke. I got that joke from Jack Nathanson.

DIANA: Well no one laughed when *you* told it, Henry. And no one laughed when you delivered that diatribe against Israel last week at lunch.

HENRY: That wasn't supposed to be funny.

DIANA: Well it certainly wasn't.

HENRY: I mean, when you think how we let one small country so totally dominate our foreign policy—

DIANA: Henry!

HENRY: Well I mean it's insane! It's suicidal! Pericles warned us about it in 426 B.C.: "Beware of entanglements in Asia Minor," he said.

DIANA: Henry, Dick Livingston was sitting right across the *table* when you said those things!

HENRY: Is Dick Jewish?

DIANA: *I'm* Jewish, Henry.

HENRY: *You're* Jewish?

DIANA: Half Jewish. My mother was an Austrian Jew.

HENRY: I didn't know that.

DIANA: Well I am. And Judy Miller is Jewish. *(Pause)*

HENRY: Has she complained that I'm prejudiced?

DIANA: No. *She* hasn't . . .

HENRY: But you still think I'm some raving neo-Nazi who is pumping anti-Semitic propaganda into his courses three times a week?

DIANA: *(Quietly)* No. I think you're a passionate teacher and scholar, whose lectures are loaded with extravagant analogies which are occasionally misinterpreted by sensitive Jewish students.

HENRY: And the Provost?

DIANA: The Provost thinks it's an issue which should never even arise. Seeing as how we're in the middle of a major fund drive. And more and more, it seems to be Jewish generosity that's keeping us all afloat.

HENRY: *(Thinking)* I do the Auerbach thing at the beginning of the term.

DIANA: The Auerbach thing?

HENRY: A great scholar. Jewish, Diana. And superb! He sees two fundamental themes in Western culture. The Greek and the Hebraic. Odysseus versus Abraham. Public honor versus private conscience.

DIANA: Well maybe that starts you off on the wrong foot.

HENRY: No, no. It works marvelously. I carry it further. I build to the basic contrast between Athens and Jerusalem.

DIANA: Well maybe those generalizations could be taken the wrong way.

HENRY: Do you think so?

DIANA: Henry: This is a free country. And academic life is even more so. You may write four-letter words all over the blackboard. You may denounce the government, blaspheme God, take off your clothes . . .

HENRY: Good Heavens, Diana . . .

DIANA: You may do all of these things in here, and most of them out there. But there is one thing, here and there, you may not do. You may *not* be insensitive about the Jews. That is taboo. The twentieth century is still with us, Henry. We live in the shadow of the Holocaust. Remember that, please. And be warned. *(Pause)*

HENRY: I hear you, Diana.

DIANA: Thank you.

HENRY: I'll stay simply with the Greeks. I'll lash myself to the mast, and avoid the Bible. I'll even avoid the Book of Job.

DIANA: Thank you, Henry.

HENRY: I must say, Diana, I've never really understood the Old Testament anyway. All that brooding, internal self-laceration. And the sense of a special contract with God. The sense of being chosen. The sense of sure salvation somewhere on down the line. Have you ever felt that? I haven't. But the Jews must feel it. Even after Auschwitz, they feel it. Perhaps because of Auschwitz, they feel it all the more. I suppose that's why they put so much stock in their children. They spoil them, you know. Their children are generally spoiled. They bring them to dinner parties. They teach them to feel—what is that word?— "entitled." Perhaps that's why this girl, excuse me, this woman, this Miss Miller, feels so strongly she deserves special treatment.

DIANA: Henry.

HENRY: My children don't feel that way. I taught my children to tow the mark. To take their turn. To submit to authority. Of course, that hasn't worked out so well either. I mean, I don't hear from my children much anymore. The Jews hear from their children. Their children telephone them all the time. *(Turns to her)* I'm painting myself into a corner, aren't I?

DIANA: Yes you are, Henry.

HENRY: Yes. Well. You're right. All this could be . . . misinterpreted. I'll try to be more careful.

DIANA: Yes, I would, Henry. Because the Provost is talking about cutting back.

HENRY: Cutting back?

DIANA: On courses that are—undersubscribed.

HENRY: My course on tragedy is required!

DIANA: Your course is on a *list* of *several* required courses. And the Provost can take it off that list any time.

HENRY: What? Tear from the Tree of Knowledge one of the last golden apples that still remain? A course that survived the ghastly chaos of the sixties? A course that—

DIANA: Henry, he can do it.

HENRY: I'll be more careful . . . "Whom the Gods would destroy, they first drive mad."

DIANA: Yes, well, and it might be a good idea, Henry—just to avoid any misunderstanding—to give Judy Miller a grade for what she's done. *(Pause)*

HENRY: You *think* so?

DIANA: Yes I do. Otherwise you might come out of this whole thing looking very much like Creon in that damn play.

HENRY: This is not a tragedy by Sophocles, Diana. It is a comedy by Aristophanes, at best. I am not Creon, and that little Jewish princess is not Antigone, Princess of Thebes.

DIANA: Cool it, Henry!

HENRY: *(With great reluctance)* I'll give her a D. For Determination.

DIANA: Henry . . .

HENRY: *(Angrily)* All right, A C, then. For Commitment.

DIANA: I don't think she'll accept a C.

HENRY: Won't *accept?*

DIANA: She feels she deserves a good grade.

HENRY: She'll get a good grade when she shows me some small awareness of what tragedy is. Lord know she's shown me what it isn't.

(JUDY *comes out now.* SHE *sits on some steps or a bench D., takes a spiral notebook out of her backpack, and writes in it, concentratedly.* DIANA *sighs and gets up.*)

DIANA: If I were you, Henry, I'd head for the hills of New Hampshire after your last class. I wouldn't want to be around when the grades go in and that play goes on and that girl doesn't graduate. Go up to your cottage, chop wood, disconnect the telephone.

HENRY: I don't like to go up there alone.

DIANA: Oh dear. Trouble again?

HENRY: Elsa's moved out. Again.

DIANA: She'll be back.

HENRY: I don't think so. She says now the children have gone, I'm impossible to live with.

DIANA: Now where did she get an idea like that?

(SHE *goes out.* HENRY *exits, after a moment, another way. The lights come up more fully on Judy, hard at her writing on the steps in the sun.* DAVE *comes on carrying a paperback book.*)

DAVE: Hi.

JUDY: (*Looking up from her work*) Hey, aren't you supposed to be in Chemistry?

DAVE: Missed it. Lost track of the time.

JUDY: But you flunked the last quiz.

DAVE: I got hung up reading one of your books.

JUDY: Which one?

DAVE: (*Showing her*) Sophocles . . . *Antigone.*

JUDY: Oh. (*Pause*)

DAVE: It's good.

JUDY: It's fair.

DAVE: It's awesome.

JUDY: It's good.

DAVE: Maybe we should do that version.

JUDY: What about mine?

DAVE: Maybe you'd get your A if you did Sophocles.

JUDY: I've thought about that, Dave: In Sophocles, all she wants to do is bury one dead brother.

DAVE: True.

JUDY: In mine, she sees everyone in the *world* as her brother, and she's fighting to keep them all *alive.*

DAVE: O.K., Jude (HE *sits down beside her, takes out a banana.)*
Want some?

JUDY: No thanks.

DAVE: *(As he eats)* While I was reading, your dad called.

JUDY: Again?

DAVE: From the hospital. Between patients.

JUDY: What did he want?

DAVE: He wants you to graduate.

JUDY: I'll graduate.

DAVE: He wants to be sure.

JUDY: Did you tell him I'm appealing to the Grievance Committee? Did you say that the Dean herself is presenting my case?

DAVE: He said committees make him nervous.

JUDY: Well, parents make *me* nervous.

DAVE: He said he hasn't spent thirty years in the lower intestine just so his daughter could flunk college.

JUDY: Sounds familiar.

DAVE: He said write the paper. Get the degree. Argue with the professor after.

JUDY: That's my father.

DAVE: That's everyone's father.

JUDY: Actually, I got a letter from my mother today.

DAVE: Coordinated attack, huh.

JUDY: She wrote from her office. On her "Department of Mental Health" stationery. Saying I was just acting out my guilt for being so lucky in life.

DAVE: You are lucky.

JUDY: I know, and I know they've worked hard to keep it that way. Moving to Westport, so I could grow up in a "healthy suburban environment." Sending me to Andover, so I could frolic in preppy heaven. Europe last summer, so I could learn how to use a credit card. Hell, four years *here*, for God's sake. And now they're offering to pay a psychiatrist two hundred dollars a week so I can blame it all on them.

DAVE: You're kidding!

JUDY: My mother even enclosed a note from my grand-mother saying that Jewish people should bend over back-wards not to make waves.

DAVE: Got you surrounded, huh?

JUDY: Sure have.

DAVE: They all just want you to do well.

JUDY: I know that. I appreciate that.

DAVE: Look. Why not hedge your bets? Do the play *and* write the paper.

JUDY: I *can't*, Dave. I've tried and I can't. It all comes out fake and phony and not me.

DAVE: Then take the C. The Dean says Harper will give you that. Take it, and run.

JUDY: I can't do that either.

DAVE: Why *not?*

JUDY: I don't know, Dave. Here I am working with a bunch of really dedicated people . . . trying to reach out to the local community . . . on a subject which deals with the survival of the entire planet . . . don't you think that's worth a tad more than a C, Dave?

DAVE: Sure it is.

JUDY: Then let me go for it.

DAVE: O.K. Let's rehearse.
(HE *tosses the banana peel into a trash can with a basketball leap.*)

JUDY: Thanks, Dave.
(SHE *hugs him.*)
    Listen to this new stuff.
(SHE *reads what she had just written.*)
    "Lately I'm feeling very much alone.
    Even you, Lysander, seem to be backing off,
    Advising caution, counseling compromise."

DAVE: *(Reading over her shoulder.)*
    "I just don't want to see you get in trouble.
    Just think what they could do to you, Antigone:
    They could throw you in jail, there to be beaten up
    By roving gangs of angry lesbians.
    Or worse:
    They could banish you, and send you off
    With no degree to grace your resume
    To fritter away essential earning years
    In waitressing or joining a typing pool."

JUDY: *(Reading)*
"Still, my conscience tells me I am right.
And if I am to suffer—"
(SHE stops; looks at him.)

DAVE: What's the matter?

JUDY: Maybe I *am* just being a brat.

DAVE: No, no . . .

JUDY: A spoiled little JAP, playing sixties-type games as a last gasp before facing up to the real world . . .

DAVE: Naa . . . .

JUDY: Maybe I should just take a massive all-nighter in the library, and grunt out one of those boring, studenty papers with a title like "Tragic Irony in Sophocles" or some such thing.

DAVE: Sounds good to me. Want me to help?

JUDY: You don't have time. *(Looking at her notebook; reading)*
"And yet this stupid arms race still goes on.
Oh it appalls me! God, it makes me mad!
(SHE begins to gather steam.)
It's as if the United States and Soviet Russia
Were two small boys comparing penises
With the fate of the world dependent on the outcome!"

DAVE: *(Covering his crotch)* Right on, Antigone!

JUDY: *(Cranking up)*
"Oh men, men, men!
Why are you all—with only a few exceptions—
(A glance at Dave)
So miserably hung up on competition?
The Air Force General, the Corporation Executive,
The College Professor tyrannizing his students . . ."

DAVE: *(Looking over her shoulder)* Hey! Where's that line? I don't see that.

JUDY: I'm improvising! I'm winging it!
"The College Professor tyrannizing his students,
It seems the entire world is under the thumb
Of self-important men. I fear, Lysander,
That one of these days, one of these little men
Will reach across his desk and push the button
Which will destroy us all!"

DAVE: Now that's pretty good.

JUDY: *(Gathering up her stuff)* No it isn't. And you know it
isn't. But I'll make it better.
(SHE starts off.)

DAVE: *(Starting after her)* I'll give you a hand.

JUDY: You better make up that chemistry. There's no reason for you to flunk out, even if I do.
(SHE goes.)

DAVE: *(Calling after her)* But I really want to—
*(HE looks at the Sophocles still in his hand, gets an idea,
concludes quietly.)* Help.
*(HE goes off the opposite way as HENRY enters to teach his
class. HE carries an old, worn leather book, stuffed with
scraps of paper. He might use half-lens reading glasses, so
that he can peer out at the audience as necessary.)*

HENRY: It might be particularly appropriate at this point in
the course to let Sophocles speak for himself. I will try to
translate for you—directly from the Greek—portions of the
great choral ode from *Antigone*. I will attempt to make
it speak as immediately as I can. And I hope, as you hear
it, you will compare it to other local efforts on this subject
that may have come to your attention in recent weeks.
*(Opening his book, finding his place, translating with great
feeling)*
"There are many wondrous things in the world,
But nothing is more wondrous than Man."
(Looks up) Deinos . . . "wondrous" . . . the other day I
heard one of you use the word "awesome." All right.
Let's try *awesome. (Returns to text.)*

"Nothing is more awesome than Man."
(Looks up: sighs) Or yes. All right. Today: woman. The point is nothing is more awesome than the human being. Here I used to contrast this awesome view with the rather abject and quarrelsome vision of man emerging in the Old Testament. But I won't do that now. Rather, returning to the text. . . . *(HE does.)* I will simply call your attention to the series of magnificent images on the taming of nature: ships, plows, fishnets, ox-yokes . . .
(Looks up) Today planes, rockets, computers, laser beams . . . *(Returns to text)*
"which man has created through his uncanny technology."
(Looks up) And then come our social inventions, those things we have invented to tame ourselves . . . *(Translates)*
"language which leads to thought" . . . "laws" . . . "medicine" . . . "religion" . . . "cities" . . . *(Looks up)* There it is. The city. The *polis*. The human community. The result of all this creative activity. We'll come back to that. *(Translates)*
"Man—or woman—is resourceful in everything, and proudly prepares for the future. *But . . .*"
(Looks up) There is a big But here . . . *But . . .* *(Translates)*
"There is one thing he can't tame, can't control: and that is Death."
(Looks up) All right now, death was terrifying—the Greeks loved life—but Sophocles goes on to mention something *worse* than death. *(Looks at text)* and here comes the crack of the whip: *(Translates grimly)*
"Yet if, for the sake of pride, he . . .
(Looks up; is glad to use the feminine this time) Or *she* . . . *(Returns to text)*
"Goes too far, then he becomes an exile . . ."
(Looks up) Which to the Greek was far, far worse than death.
(Translates)
"An exile without a country,
Lost and alone,
Homeless and outlawed forever."

You see? Sophocles joyfully celebrates the lawful human community, the Greek *polis*, but then threatens those who defy it with a death beyond death—exile, banishment, ostracism. *(Returns to the text)*
"Lost and alone.
Homeless and outlawed forever."
(Looks up) Last year, I compared these grim lines to the Hebrew's lamentations in the Psalms. This year, I will try to conjure up other images of profound alienation: (HE *thinks.)* The haunted Orestes . . . Napoleon dying his slow death on the desolate island of Saint Helena . . . some lost astronaut severed forever from the good, green earth . . . *(Returns to the text)*
"Homeless and outlawed forever."
(Pause) Those words were written over two thousand years ago. I have read and taught them countless times. I get shivers up and down my spine every time I do. *(The bell rings.* HE *closes his book.)* I think even Sophocles would commend my theatrical timing. For the next session, read *The Trojan Women* by Euripides. Feminists will appreciate his sympathetic portrayal of women. Pacifists will admire his bitter attack on war. Classicists, however, prefer to reach beyond such limited responses. Thank you, and good afternoon. (HE *gathers his books as* DAVE *approaches him.)*

DAVE: Professor Harper?

HENRY: *(Turning)* Yes?

DAVE: I'm a friend of Judy's.

HENRY: Judy?

DAVE: Miss Miller.

HENRY: Ah.

DAVE: *(Holding out envelope)* She asked me to give you this.

HENRY: "Has she sent poison or some other implement of dark death?"

DAVE: Excuse me?

HENRY: A line from *Medea.*

DAVE: It's just her term paper.

HENRY: She should be in class. She should hand it in herself.

DAVE: I think she's—a little mad at you, sir.

HENRY: Mad? At me? Because I want her to learn? Oh dear. Would you tell her, please, that the quest for truth and beauty is a slow and painful climb, and she shouldn't bite the hand that leads her. *(His little pun)*

DAVE: I'll—tell her something.

HENRY: Good. Meanwhile, I'll take that paper, in hopes she soon will return to the fold.

DAVE: Thank you, sir.

HENRY: *(Opening the envelope, sliding the paper out far enough to read the title)* "Tragic Irony in Sophocles' *Antigone.*" A good, no-nonsense title.

DAVE: I'll tell her, sir. (HE *starts off.)*

HENRY: *(Pulling the paper out of the envelope)* Lovely looking paper . . . Well typed.

DAVE: Mmm.

HENRY: Is this an electric typewriter?

DAVE: No actually, it's a word processor.

HENRY: She can't come to class, but she seems to have found time to form a relationship with a computer.

DAVE: Actually, I did the typing, sir.

HENRY: Well let's hope the contents are as attractive as the form. (HE *starts to thumb through the papers.)*

DAVE: I'll be going, then. (HE *starts off.)*

HENRY: *(As he reads; calling out)* Oh, ah, Mr.—

DAVE: *(Stopping; turning)* Dave.

HENRY: Do you have a moment?

DAVE: Well I—

HENRY: Would you be so kind as to accompany me to my office?

DAVE: Me?

HENRY: If you would.

DAVE: Now?

HENRY: If you'd be so kind.
(HE *turns and crosses slowly toward his office, still reading the paper.* DAVE *hesitates a moment, and then follows.* HENRY *enters his office, and sits at his desk, still reading.* DAVE *stands in the doorway. As he reads, gesturing vaguely.)*
Please sit down, Mr. . . . ah . . .

DAVE: Dave.

HENRY: Sit down, please.

DAVE: Thank you.
(HE *sits on the edge of the chair.* HENRY *continues to read.* DAVE *watches him.)*

HENRY: *(As he reads)* This . . . appears to be . . . an excellent paper.

DAVE: Is it?

HENRY: *(Thumbing through to the end)* Even a cursory glance tells me it's first-rate.

DAVE: I'll tell her, sir.

HENRY: I've been around a long time. I've taught this course a good many years. I know a good paper when I see one, and I see one here.

DAVE: *(Almost at the door)* That's great, sir.

HENRY: *(Quietly)* Who wrote it?

DAVE: Huh?

HENRY: Who wrote this paper?

DAVE: Judy wrote it.

HENRY: No she didn't. I've also been around long enough to know that. She wrote a promising little essay for me at the start of the semester. She wrote a rather breathless hour exam. But she did not write this. She is not yet capable of the care and commitment I see emerging here.

DAVE: Maybe she's changed, sir.

HENRY: Ah. Then I would like to discuss this paper with her. Would you get her, please?

DAVE: I think she's rehearsing, sir.

HENRY: Then I must ask you to seek her out. Tell her I am passionate to engage in an intensive discussion with a kindred classicist.

DAVE: Sir . . .

HENRY: You might also tell her, *en passant*, that I think this is plagiarism, pure and simple. She has tried to pass off as her own the work of somebody else. This is an offense punishable, according to the rules, by . . . *(HE has found the college rule book and is already thumbing through it. HE finds his place.)* "Automatic failure of the course involved."

DAVE: Sir . . .

HENRY: *(Reading)* "*And*, after due deliberation by the Discipline Committee, possible expulsion from the University." *(Pause. HE looks at DAVE.)*

DAVE: *(Quietly)* Oh boy.

HENRY: You might also be interested in the fact that . . .
(HE reads again from the book.) "persons aiding or contributing to a plagiaristic act will similarly be charged and punished." *(Looks up)*

You personally might be interested in that, Mr.—?

DAVE: Appleton.

HENRY: Well I'm not going to press charges against you. Mr. Appleton.

DAVE: Sir—

HENRY: Nor am I going to press charges against Miss Miller. Believe it or not, I would hate to prevent her from graduating. I would simply ask you to tell her to make an appointment at her earliest convenience, so that I may explain to her why, in the world of scholarship and learning, plagiarism is a dark and bloody crime. *(DAVE stands at the door.)* That's all I have to say. You may go.

DAVE: She didn't write it.

HENRY: *(Infinitely patient)* Yes I know. That's what I've been saying.

DAVE: No, I mean she doesn't even know about it.

HENRY: Doesn't know?

DAVE: She still wants her play to be her paper. *(Pause)*

HENRY: Then who wrote this?

DAVE: I did.

HENRY: Unbeknownst to her?

DAVE: Yes, sir.

HENRY: Hoping I'd give it a good grade, and she'd go along with it, and the problem would be solved?

DAVE: I don't know what I hoped. *(Pause)*

HENRY: *(Looking at paper again)* And where did you get this paper? From some other student at some other college? From one of those companies who accept money and do your research?

DAVE: No! I wrote it myself.

HENRY: I don't believe that.

DAVE: Well I did.

HENRY: How could you? You're not in my course.

DAVE: I still wrote it.
(Pause. HENRY *looks at the paper, looks at* DAVE.*)*

HENRY: Sit down, please.
*(*DAVE *does.* HENRY *is now all business.)*
Name three plays by Sophocles beside the *Antigone.*

DAVE: *Oedipus Rex, Oedipus at Colonnus . . . Ajax.*

HENRY: Describe Antigone's geneology.

DAVE: Her father was Oedipus. Her mother, Jocasta. Her sister was Ismene. She had two brothers. Eteocles and Polynices. *(Pause)* Who killed each other. *(Pause)* Fighting. *(Pause)* For the throne. *(Pause)* Of Thebes. *(Pause)*

HENRY: And what, briefly, do you think *is* the "Tragic Irony in Sophocles' *Antigone*"?

DAVE: I don't think it's Antigone's tragedy at all. I think it's Creon's.

HENRY: And why do you think that?

DAVE: Because she at least wins her point in the end.

HENRY: She dies.

DAVE: But she wins. He loses. Everything. The Gods are much more unfair to him. *(Pause)*

HENRY: You're very good.

DAVE: Thank you.

HENRY: Where did you learn all this?

DAVE: I read the play.

HENRY: *(Indicating paper)* No. There's more here than just that.

DAVE: My grandfather liked the Greeks.

HENRY: Was he an academic?

DAVE: No. He just liked the classics. He spent most of his spare time in the library, reading the Greeks.

HENRY: And he taught you?

DAVE: Right. And I kept it up when I had time.

HENRY: I could never get my own son to read anything but science fiction.

DAVE: That's what my dad reads. *(They laugh together.)*

HENRY: Why have you never taken a course from me?

DAVE: I couldn't fit it into my schedule.

HENRY: What's your major?

DAVE: Chemistry.

HENRY: Better worlds through the chemistry, eh.

DAVE: Actually, my grades aren't too good.

HENRY: They'd be good in the classics.

DAVE: Not many jobs out there in that.

HENRY: Still, you should take my course.

DAVE: I wish I could.

HENRY: We could do a special seminar together. Study one play in depth. I'm fascinated with the *Antigone*. We could really dig in, you and I, next fall.

DAVE: I'm supposed to graduate this spring, sir.

HENRY: Oh dear . . . Then perhaps we might meet in the afternoon, from here on in. A small tutorial.

DAVE: I can't, sir. I'm on the track team.

HENRY: The track team? Splendid! The Greeks invented competitive sport!

DAVE: I know.

HENRY: *Hygies psyche meta somatos hygious.*

DAVE: Excuse me?

HENRY: We'll shift to Latin: *Mens sana in corpore sano.*

DAVE: *(Trying to translate)* Sane mind . . .

HENRY: Sound mind in a sound body. The Tenth Satire by Juvenal.

DAVE: Juvenal . . . Tenth . . .

HENRY: You don't by any chance throw the discus, do you? No, that would be too much.

DAVE: I just run the Four Hundred.

HENRY: Ah. Fleet of foot. A true Greek. "Skilled in all-ways of contending."

DAVE: Thank you, sir.

HENRY: Well, then, I wonder if I might keep on this fine paper long enough for Mrs. Murphy to make a Xerox copy.

DAVE: Sure.
(HE *gets up to leave.*)

HENRY: Just to remind me occasionally of what a good student can do.

DAVE: Sure.
(HE *starts for the door. At this point,* JUDY *enters at another part of the stage.* SHE *sits on a bench, and waits impatiently as if in a waiting room.*)

HENRY: You must be very fond of Miss Miller.

DAVE: I am.

HENRY: To have written this for her.

DAVE: I liked writing it.

HENRY: Will you be seeing her soon?

DAVE: I think so.

HENRY: Would you remind her that she and I have yet to resolve our difficulties?

DAVE: She's stubborn, sir.

HENRY: I give you permission to help her. Be her tutor. See that she gets some small awareness of Greek tragedy.

DAVE: She thinks she already has, sir.

HENRY: But she *hasn't!* She sees answers, solutions, revisions. Tell her there are things beyond the world of management which are profoundly unmanageable!

DAVE: She wouldn't listen, sir.

HENRY: Then she and I are on a collision course.

DAVE: I'm afraid so, sir.
(DAVE *starts for the door again.*)

HENRY: One more minute, please.
(DAVE *stops.*) Appleton, you said your name was?

DAVE: That's right.

HENRY: English, I suppose.

DAVE: Originally.

HENRY: The English love the classics.

DAVE: Yes.

HENRY: And Miss Miller's Jewish.

DAVE: That's right.

HENRY: May I speak classicist to classicist?

DAVE: Yeah. Sure.

HENRY: What you are witnessing here, Mr. Appleton, is once again the age-old clash between Athens and Jerusalem.

DAVE: I don't get you, sir.

HENRY: Read Tertullian. Third century, A.D. "What is Athens to Jerusalem, or Jerusalem to Athens?" There it all is. The private conscience versus the communal obligation. Jew versus Greek. Miss Miller versus me.

DAVE: You think so?

HENRY: I do, but they tell me I shouldn't.

DAVE: It seems a little . . . exaggerated, sir.

HENRY: You're probably right.
(HENRY *gets up; takes his arm.*)
Come, I'll walk with you down the hall. Plato and Aristotle, strolling through the colonnades of academe. We'll discuss simply Sophocles.

DAVE: O.K.

HENRY: *(As they go)* And I hope Miss Miller appreciates this grand gesture you made on her behalf.

DAVE: God, I hope she never finds out about it.
(THEY *go out as* DIANA *comes on, carrying a folder.* JUDY *gets up expectantly)*

JUDY: Well?

DIANA: The meeting's over.

JUDY: And?

DIANA: *(Deep breath)* The Grievance Committee voted against you, Judy.

JUDY: *Against?*

DIANA: I'm sorry. *(They move into her office.)*

JUDY: Did the students on the committee vote against me?

DIANA: I can't reveal the specific vote.

JUDY: How about you? How did you vote?

DIANA: I abstained, of course. Since I was presenting your case.

JUDY: How would you have voted? If you could have? *(Pause)*

DIANA: Against.

JUDY: What?!

DIANA: I put your case as fairly as I could, Judy. Really. But your argument simply didn't hold. The committee felt you were asking them to violate the integrity of the classroom. You want them to intrude on a principle that goes back to the Middle Ages.

JUDY: But other people do it all the time! There's guy in Geology who got partial credit for skiing down Mount Washington!

DIANA: I know . . .

JUDY: And there's a girl who passed her Chemistry lab by cooking a crabmeat casserole.

DIANA: I know that, and I think it's disgraceful. But those are other instructors. We cannot dictate standards to *any* professor. You signed up for Greek tragedy. You bought the books. You read the syllabus. You agreed in effect to submit to the rules. There it is.

JUDY: There is it. Everyone seems to be backing off these days. You, my family, now the committee.

DIANA: Oh, Judy . . .

JUDY: *(Almost in tears)* I guess I'm doomed to be alone.

DIANA: What about all those people working on your play?

JUDY: It's just extracurricular to them. I'm the one who's really on the line.

DIANA: Well what about that boy you go with?

JUDY: Oh, he just loves me, that's all.

DIANA: *(lighting a cigarette)* Well I'm sorry, Judy. I did what I could.

JUDY: Please don't smoke!

DIANA: I'm sorry.

JUDY: I think I'm allergic to it.

DIANA: All right, Judy.

JUDY: And it violates my air space.

DIANA: *(Putting cigarettes away)* All right, all right. *(Pause)*

JUDY: So what do I do?

DIANA: I told you: he's offered a C.

JUDY: I'm beyond a C.

DIANA: Beyond?

JUDY: I can't settle for a C.

DIANA: Then you won't graduate.

JUDY: Not in June. No.

DIANA: That's ridiculous!

JUDY: I'll make it up in summer school with that course on comedy where all they do is study *Annie Hall*. You can mail me my degree in September.

DIANA: That makes me a little angry, Judy. You told me you wanted to stand up with your class.

JUDY: I'm standing up, all right.

DIANA: But you'll lose your job! It depends on your graduating.

JUDY: I'll find another.

DIANA: That's not so easy these days.

JUDY: What's a job anyway? Is it the most important thing in the world? I suppose this is a hopelessly middle-class thing to say, but am I supposed to live and die over a job? Do you? You've been here a long time, worked your way up, now you're Dean of the whole department. Is that *it*? Are you in heaven now? Aren't there other things in your life beside your job?

DIANA: *(Taken aback)* Of course there are, Judy . . .

JUDY: I mean, that's all I cared about, once upon a time. A *job*. I couldn't wait until I was scampering up and down Wall Street in my gray and white Adidas and a new suit from Saks, with my little leather briefcase swinging by my side. Meeting men for lunch and women for dinner, and both in the Health Club afterwards. A co-op on the East Side with a VCR and an answering machine with a funny message. Weekends at Sugarbush and Vineyard. Vacations in the Bahamas and France. Nailing down forty or fifty thou per annum within three years. Moving onward and upward through the corridors of power until I get an office with a corner view where I can look down on millions of women scampering up and down Wall Street in their gray and white Adidas.

DIANA: That's not the worst thing in the world!

JUDY: Isn't it? I'm not so sure. I'm beginning to think it's a con deal. All us women now killing ourselves to do those things that a lot of men decided not to do twenty years ago. I mean, here we are, the organization women, punching the clock, flashing the credit card, smoking our lungs out, while the really smart men are off making furniture or playing the clarinet or something. Look at you. Do you really want to be Dean, or are you just making some sort of feminist statement?

DIANA: Let's leave me out of this, please.

JUDY: Well all I know is I'm not so hung up on "The Job" anymore. It just seems like more of the same. More of what I did at Andover and at Westport Junior High before that. More of what I've done every summer, with my creative camps and internships and my special sum-

mer projects. Touching all the bases, following all the
rules, ever since I can remember. And now here I am,
about to graduate, or rather *not* graduate, because I've
come up with the first vaguely unselfish idea I've ever
had in my life, and this place, this institution—in which
my family has invested at least seventy thousand dollars—
won't give me credit for it.

DIANA: A C is a decent grade, Judy. We used to call
it a gentleman's C.

JUDY: Well I'm no gentleman.
(SHE starts out.)

DIANA: Judy . . . One more thing.
(JUDY stops, turns.)

JUDY: What?

DIANA: The Provost sat in on the Grievance Committee
meeting.

JUDY And?

DIANA: After it was over, he took me aside. He asked me
to ask you a question.

JUDY: Go ahead.

DIANA: . . . The Provost wondered if your difficulty with
Professor Harper has anything to do with . . . ethnic
issues.

JUDY: Say again?

DIANA: A student has recently complained that Professor
Harper is anti-Semitic?

JUDY: Anti-Se*mi*tic?

DIANA: That's the complaint.

JUDY: Anti-Semitic? It's probably that Talmudic type who
sits in the front row and argues about everything. I bet
he wears his yarmulke even in the shower.

DIANA: Ah, but you don't feel that way?

JUDY: No way.

DIANA: Oh, Judy, I'm so glad to hear it.

JUDY: I never even thought of it.

DIANA: Good. Then I'll tell the Provost.

JUDY: I mean should I worry about that? My grandmother says you have to watch out for that sort of thing at all times.

DIANA: Yes well, times change.

JUDY: Unless it's there, and I didn't see it.

DIANA: No, no . . .

JUDY: I mean, maybe I'm so assimilated into white-bread middle-class America that it passed me right by. Maybe I should reexamine this whole issue with that in mind. Thanks a lot, Dean!
(SHE goes out.)

DIANA: *(Calling after her)* Judy! Judy! . . . Oh God!
(SHE makes up her mind, opens a desk drawer, takes out a small tape recorder which she slams onto the desk. SHE pushes the buttons determinedly and then begins to dictate, pacing around her office as she smokes. Dictating.)
Monica, please type a letter to the Provost . . . Dear Walter . . . I herewith submit my resignation as Dean, to be effective at the end of this school year. I find I long to return to the clear lines and concrete issues of the classroom. I especially yearn to resume my studies of Jane Austen, and the subordinate role of women in the eighteenth century. I will miss, of course, the sense of bustle and activity I've found here in Administration. There's something to be said, after all, for the friendships which come from working closely with other people during regular hours—among which I count my friendship with the other Deans, and you, Walter, and Monica, my fine assistant . . . Indeed, in some ways, I dread retreating to

the hermetic world of bickering colleagues, sullen students, hopeless meetings, long hours of preparation . . . *(SHE slows down.)* . . . the loneliness of the library . . . the meals alone . . . the sense that something more important is going on everywhere else in the world . . . *(Long pause)* Just type a rough draft of this, Monica. I'll look at it tomorrow. *(SHE clicks off the tape recorder, puts it back in her desk. DAVE enters in a track suit, starts doing stretch exercises. DIANA crosses to doorway, calls off.)* Monica, see if you can locate Professor Harper . . . *(Then SHE takes some computer printout sheets out of her briefcase and begins to go over them at her desk as the lights dim on her. The lights come up more fully on DAVE, doing stretch exercises. We hear the distant sounds of students cheering. JUDY comes on. It is by now late enough in the spring so she doesn't wear a jacket.)*

JUDY: Dave . . . *(SHE hugs him from behind.)*

DAVE: *(Through his stretches; pantingly)* Hi . . .

JUDY: Am I bothering you?

DAVE: *(Grunting; stretching)* Yes . . . But that's O.K.

JUDY: I Just want to tell you something, David.

DAVE: *(Still exercising.)* Uh oh. When it's David, it's serious.

JUDY: I just want to tell you not to memorize any more of those speeches.

DAVE: Thank God.

JUDY: I'm changing everything.

DAVE: Again?

JUDY: I'm starting all over. From scratch.

DAVE: Why?

JUDY: I didn't like what we had. I can do better.

DAVE: Yeah?

JUDY: Now I'm on a totally different track. I mean, it's still *Antigone*. But I'm adding a whole new dimension.

DAVE: Are you throwing in acid rain?

JUDY: *(Laughing)* No. I'm onto something much deeper. *(A whistle is heard offstage.* DAVE *starts off.)*

DAVE: There's the Four Hundred. I've got to go.

JUDY: So throw away the old stuff.

DAVE: Is there a lot new to learn?

JUDY: Mostly for me.

DAVE: Can you tell me where you're taking it?

JUDY: Well I'm striving for a more natural style.

DAVE: Way to go.

JUDY: And I'm connecting my attack on nuclear armaments with the issue of meaningful work.

DAVE: Excellent.

JUDY: And I'm making Antigone Jewish.
(SHE goes off. Another whistle from offstage. HE looks after her, then runs off the opposite way as . . . the lights come up on DIANA, who is still at her desk, working on printout sheets. After a moment, HENRY appears in the doorway. He watches her affectionately for a moment.)

HENRY: *(Finally)* Woman at her work. I am reminded of Penelope at her loom.

DIANA: *(Looking up: quickly putting away the sheets)* Come in, Henry.

HENRY: *(Coming in)* What a magnificent office, Diana! What corporate dimensions *(As* DIANA *puts her cigarette out)* Thank you . . . A view of the Charles! The spires of Harvard dimly seen up the river! How different it is from the monkish cells assigned to those of us who teach.

DIANA: You've been here before, Henry.

HENRY: Never. I've scrupulously avoided all official contact with the bureaucracy, except on my own turf. I wouldn't be here now, dear Diana, but for a series of rather frantic telephone messages left under my door. (HE *takes a stack of pink slips out of his pocket, reads.)* Call the Dean . . . See the Dean . . . Please call or see the Dean.

DIANA: Sit down, Henry.

HENRY: *(Sitting)* I will, but I must warn you I have very little time. We are now deep in the last plays of Euripides, particularly the *Bacchae*, which I continually find to be one of the more profoundly disturbing works of man. He has an even darker vision than Sophocles.

DIANA: Well maybe I've got some news that will cheer you up, Henry.

HENRY: Beware of Deans bearing gifts.

DIANA: Remember the grant you applied for two years ago?

HENRY: Ah yes. To go to Greece. To see the restorations at Epidaurus. *(Pause)* And to restore a ruin or two in my own life.

DIANA: Well you've got that grant now, Henry.

HENRY: Now?

DIANA: I've been talking to the Provost. He's giving you next year off. All year. At full pay.

HENRY: Are you serious?

DIANA: I'm always serious, Henry. That's my problem, in case you ever notice. *(Pause)*

HENRY: Why suddenly now?

DIANA: Ours not to reason why, Henry.

HENRY: I begged for that leave two years ago. I practically fell to my knees and supplicated the Provost like old Priam before Achilles. I thought if Elsa and I could just get away . . .

DIANA: Call her. Tell her you've lucked out, at long last.

HENRY: It's too late. She's . . . found someone. Apparently they sit and hold hands and watch television. Anyway, she wants a divorce.

DIANA: I am sorry.

HENRY: No, no, it's good. It's very good. The other shoe has dropped. Finally.

DIANA: Take one of your children then. Give them a trip.

HENRY: They wouldn't come. *(Pause)* They have their own lives. *(Pause)* Such as they are. *(Quietly)* I'll go alone. *(Pause; HE looks at her)* Unless you'd come with me.

DIANA: Henry!

HENRY: Why not? Take a sabbatical. You're overdue.

DIANA: You mean, just—blip out into the blue Aegean?

HENRY: Exactly! Spend a naughty year abroad with an old satyr. Tell you what, I'd even let you smoke.

DIANA: I think I'd give it up if I went abroad.

HENRY: Then there we are!

DIANA: Oh gosh! To get away! To see something else besides these—walls! Just think, Henry . . . *(SHE stops.)* Just think. *(Pause. Sadly.)* It wouldn't work, Henry.

HENRY: It might.

DIANA: It already didn't, Henry. On that strange weekend in that gloomy hotel during the M.L.A. conference.

HENRY: That was a lovely weekend.

DIANA: It was not.

HENRY: Dido and Aeneas in their enchanted cave . . .

DIANA: Oh Henry, *please*!

HENRY: What's the matter?

DIANA: Dido, Penelope, Clytemnestra! I am not a *myth*, Henry! I am not a *meta*phor!

HENRY: My dear lady . . .

DIANA: No, no, I'm *me*, Henry! I live and breathe in my own right! Do you know anything about my *life?* Do you know where I live? Do you know I have a daughter in junior high?

HENRY: Of course I know you have . . .

DIANA: What's her name, Henry? What's my daughter's *name?* It's not Electra and it's not Athena and it's not . . .

HENRY: Let me think . . .

DIANA: You don't *know*, Henry. And you don't know that my mother died last semester, and you don't know that I used to play the French horn. You don't *see* me, Henry. You don't see anyone. In your mind, everything is an example of something else! I suppose it's called stereotyping, but whatever it is, I don't like it, Henry! It makes me feel insignificant and unreal.

HENRY: Diana, dear friend . . .
(HE *moves toward her.*)

DIANA: No, now stay away from me, Henry. Don't touch me. Go to *Greece*, for God's sake! Find some young woman—excuse me, some sea nymph—who will throw herself into your arms on the topless shores of Mykenos. Really. Just go.
(Pause)

HENRY: Tell the Provost I'll take a raincheck.

DIANA: A raincheck?

HENRY: Maybe in a year or two. When my life is more in order.

DIANA: It doesn't work that way, Henry. It's now or not at all.

HENRY: Then I'll have to forego it.

DIANA: Oh Henry . . .

HENRY: At this point in my life, I need my classes. Strange as that may seem.
(HE *starts out.*)
And now, if you'll excuse me, the *Bacchae* call me to the dance.

DIANA: Henry! (HE *stops.*) Other things go on in this university at the end of the school year besides discussions of the *Bacchae.*

HENRY: *(Stopping, turning)* Such as?

DIANA: *(Taking the computer printouts from her desk)* Well, for example, Henry, there's something called preregistration, when students give an indication of what courses they'd like to take next fall.

HENRY: The annual body count.

DIANA: *(Indicating sheets)* Exactly, Henry. And we in the Humanities are down.

HENRY: We are always down. We are doomed to be down. We live in an age where a book—a good book—is as obsolete as an Aeolian harp. All the more reason to keep standards *up*.

DIANA: You, particularly, are down, Henry. *(Pause)*

HENRY: How many did I get?

DIANA: Two.

HENRY: Two? Two next fall? Two students to take through the entire rise and fall of the Roman Empire.

DIANA: Two, Henry.

HENRY: How many for my elective on Plato?

DIANA: Four.

HENRY: Four. Two for Rome, four for Plato. Six students, next fall, out of over four thousand, have shown some interest in the classical tradition. This, in a country founded by Washington and Jefferson and Madison precisely to reestablish that tradition.

DIANA: Shakespeare, on the other hand, is up.

HENRY: I must say, Diana, I fail to understand why students choose what they do. They land on courses like starlings on a telephone wire. It seems totally random.

DIANA: The Provost is cancelling all undergraduate courses with an enrollment of less than five, Henry.

HENRY: What?

DIANA: The Provost is cancelling your courses.

HENRY: He has no right!

DIANA: He has every right. It's a budgetary thing. There are clear rules about it. Jack Edward's seminar on Racine goes. Sally Weiskopf's section on Keats. The history department lost the entire seventeenth century.

HENRY: I'll talk to him. These things can change. Students can sign up in the fall.

DIANA: He's laid down the law, Henry. Jack Edwards has already gone up and been refused. *(Pause)*

HENRY: Then I'll teach something else.

DIANA: Such as what, Henry?

HENRY: Dante. I'll teach Dante. I'm beginning to get a new understanding of Hell.

DIANA: Bill Brindisi's got Dante.

HENRY: Shakespeare, then. I'll do a section of Shakespeare.

DIANA: You don't like Shakespeare.

HENRY: Of course I like Shakespeare. He's just a bit . . . messy, that's all. And a bit over-picked. I refuse to spend an entire class focussing on the button image in *King Lear*. I'll do the Roman plays: *Julius Caesar, Coriolanus* . . .

DIANA: Jane Tillotson's got Shakespeare, Henry. All of him.

HENRY: All right then, what? Tolstoy? Joyce? I'm an educated man. I can do anything. Give me the freshman course—Introduction to Literature. I'll take it over. I'll muster that motley crew of junior instructors who teach it. We'll begin with the *Iliad*, and stride down the centuries, concluding with Conrad.

DIANA: I think they *start* with Conrad in that course, Henry.

HENRY: Oh really? Well, we'll change that. We'll—

DIANA: Henry. *(Pause)* The Provost doesn't want you to teach. At all.

HENRY: Why not?

DIANA: He thinks your courses are becoming . . . problematic, Henry.

HENRY: The *Antigone* thing?

DIANA: And the anti-Semitic thing.

HENRY: I have scrupulously avoided anything controversial in my class.

DIANA: Apparently she hasn't, in her play. I hear it's more and more about being Jewish, and more and more about you.

HENRY: *(Quietly, with increasing anger)* There is a law as old as Solon which allows a man to confront his accusers. I want to meet her, right now, in front of the Provost, and you, and Ariel Sharon, if he wants to be there!

DIANA: The Provost already met with her, Henry.

HENRY: And what did she say?

DIANA: Nothing! Everything! I don't know! He said it was all very general . . . He said you both deserve each other. He said if he didn't have the alumni breathing down his neck, he'd turn you both loose in the ring, and the hell with it. But right now, all he wants to do is get her graduated and you out of the country, so that things can simmer *down*. Now go to *Greece*, Henry, and enjoy it!

HENRY: And when I come back, he'll suggest early retirement.

DIANA: He might.

HENRY: He'll sweeten the pie. Buy me off with a few impressive benefits.

DIANA: You've been here a long time, Henry. I think they'd be very generous.

HENRY: I want to teach, Diana.

DIANA: I know.

HENRY: I need to teach.

DIANA: I know, I know . . .

HENRY: It's what I do.

DIANA: Henry, my old colleague . . .

HENRY: I am a classical scholar. I trained at Harvard. I have written three good books. I know a great deal, and I have to teach what I know, and I'm only good when I'm teaching it! My wife has left me, my children have scattered, I have nothing else but this! I have to teach, Diana. Have to. Or I'm dead.

DIANA: You need students, Henry.

HENRY: Then I'll have to get them, won't I?
(HE *goes off. Diana sits there for a moment, then opens her purse, takes out a pack of cigarettes. She shakes it, but it's*

empty. SHE *gets up, and begins to walk toward the wings, calling out sweetly as she goes.)*

DIANA: Monica? . . . Did you bring any cigarettes in today? . . . Because if you did, even though you're down to your last one, I intend to get it, Monica. I intend to wrestle you to the ground!

*(*SHE *goes off, as* JUDY *comes on. She leans against a pillar in a rather theatrical pose and recites her lines, referring only occasionally to a script she carries, in her hand.)*

JUDY: "So Creon has determined I go to jail. I wonder if this is happening because I'm Jewish. I don't mean simply that Creon's prejudiced—though he probably is. I mean more because of me. Maybe it's built into my Jewish blood to rise up against the Creons of this world. All I know is for the first time in my life I've felt in tune with something larger than myself. I've been to the library lately. I've studied my roots. And I've learned how often we Jews have stood our ground against injustice. Pharaoh and Philistine, Hittite and Herod have fallen before us. Roman generals and Spanish Inquisitors, Venetian businessmen and Russian Cossacks, Nazis, Arabs, McCarthyites—all the arrogant authorities of this world have tried to subdue us. And when we protest, they throw us into jail. Well, what's jail these days? Maybe this is a jail right here. This so-called ivory tower. This labyrinth of curricular obligations. This festering nest of overpaid administrators. This rotten pit of dry and exhausted pedants. This winter camp which capitalism creates to keep its children off the job market. What job market? Where are the jobs? Where is there decent work in an economy so devoted to nonessential goods and destructive weapons?"

*(*DAVE *comes on.)*

DAVE: Judy—

JUDY: Wait. I'm almost done. *(*SHE *continues to recite.)* "Or maybe this whole damn country is a jail. Maybe we're all prisoners. Prisoners of these oppressive corporations, who capture us with their advertising, chain us to their products, and work us forever in meaningless jobs to pay for things we shouldn't even want."

DAVE: Judy. It's important.

JUDY: Hold it. (SHE *takes a deep breath.*) "And to protect this prison, this fortress America, this so-called way of life, we arm ourselves with weapons which, if they're used, could ten times over destroy the world, blot out the past, and turn the future into a desolate blank. Are we so sure we're right? Is life in these United States so great? Would the homeless hordes on the streets of New York agree? Would the hungry blacks in the South? Would the migrant workers breaking their backs to feed us go along with it? Oh God, Lysander, this might be a terrible thing to say, but I don't think our country is worth dying for any more. The world at large is worth dying for, not just us."

DAVE: Wow! That's tremendous.

JUDY: Thank you. *(Pause)*

DAVE: *(Quietly)* He wants to see you.

JUDY: The Provost? I know. I have a meeting with him in half an hour.

DAVE: No, *Harper! Harper* wants to see you.

JUDY: Harper?

DAVE: He called me at the lab.

JUDY: How come he called *you*?

DAVE: I don't know . . . I guess he knew I knew you. Anyway, he said he watched the rehearsal last night.

JUDY: *What?*

DAVE: He was there. And he wants to talk to you about it.

JUDY: Oh God. What did he think?

DAVE: Didn't say.
(The lights begin to come up on Henry's office, as HENRY *comes in, settles at his desk.)*

JUDY: Oh Lord, he must have hated it. All that Creon stuff I put in. Well, maybe it'll do him good.

DAVE: He said he'd be in his office all afternoon. You better see him.

JUDY: *(Putting on lip gloss)* I might. Then again I might not. First, of course, I have a major meeting with the Provost.
(SHE starts out.)

DAVE: *(Calling after Judy)* Hey, you're quite the Queen Bee around here these days.

JUDY: I'm another Antigone.

DAVE: Antigone dies in the end, remember.

JUDY: That's the old version. Mine ends happily ever after.
(SHE goes off.)

DAVE: *(Calling after her)* Ever hear of *hubris*, Judy? Know what that word means . . . (HE *sees she's gone; speaks to himself.)* Pride. Overweening pride. For example, take a man whose father gives him a chemistry set when he's eight years old. This man takes Chemistry in high school, and majors in it in college. What makes this man think he can graduate if he doesn't study? What makes this man think he can find a job if he doesn't graduate? What makes this man stand around, talking to himself, when his final exam in Chemistry starts in five minutes, and he doesn't know the stuff at *all?* Pride, that's what. *Hubris.* Which leads to tragedy every time. (HE *goes off grimly as the lights come up on* HENRY *in his office. After a moment,* JUDY *comes in.)*

JUDY: You wanted to see me, Professor Harper?

HENRY: *(Jumping up)* Ah. Miss Miller. Yes. *(Indicates a chair)* Please.

(JUDY *comes in.*)
How well you look.

JUDY: Thank you.

HENRY: I am reminded of a line from the *Andromache:* "I now wear different robes."

JUDY: I don't know that one.

HENRY: No matter. You look lovely. Life on the wicked stage becomes you.

JUDY: Thanks. (SHE *sits.*)

HENRY: Yes, well, now I have recently had the opportunity to watch you practice your play.

JUDY: You mean, re*hearse.*

HENRY: Yes. Rehearse. Last night, in fact. I happen to know old Bill, who's the custodian of the Spingler Auditorium, and he took me up to the back of the balcony and let me sit there unobtrusively and watch you rehearse your play.

JUDY: I heard.

HENRY: Oh yes? Well that's where I was. All evening. *(Pause)* I found it . . . *(This is tough for him.)* Interesting. *(Pause)* Quite interesting *(Pause)* The crude poetry, the naive theatricality . . .

JUDY: Thank you.

HENRY: Your work also demonstrated an earnestness and commitment which I found . . . refreshing, in a world which seems too often concerned only with the meaning of meaning.

JUDY: You mean, you *liked* it? *(Pause)*

HENRY: I . . . admired it.

JUDY: Well thank you very much! I appreciate that.

HENRY: I have decided it may substitute after all for your term paper.

JUDY: That's great!

HENRY: Miss Miller, you might be interested to know that Sophocles himself was a practical man of the theater. Not only did he write his plays, but he directed most of them, and sometimes acted in them as well, just as you are doing.

JUDY: Really?

HENRY: Absolutely. And according to Aristotle—this might amuse you—he actually danced in a lost play of his called *Nausicaa*. He danced. He danced the part of a young woman playing ball.

JUDY: No kidding! That makes me feel very proud!

HENRY: Then I wonder if you would play ball with *me*, Miss Miller.

JUDY: What do you mean?

HENRY: Well, now, last night, I noticed a number of people scurrying about, assisting with your production.

JUDY: Yes . . .

HENRY: Good, practical souls, hard at work. I mean, not only did I notice your personal and particular friend . . .

JUDY: Dave . . .

HENRY: Yes, Dave. A fine stalwart young man. I noticed him. But I also noticed other actors, and that odd cluster of people pretending to be the chorus.

JUDY: Right . . .

HENRY: And then I hear there's to be an orchestra . . .

JUDY: A group. A combo, really . . .

HENRY: Well how many do you think are involved, in toto?

JUDY: In toto?

HENRY: Altogether.

JUDY: Oh . . . maybe . . . thirty-five.

HENRY: And of course not all of them will graduate this year, will they?

JUDY: No. Some. Not all.

HENRY: Miss Miller, I wonder if you would announce to everyone in your production that I'm planning to give a special seminar next fall.

JUDY: Special seminar?

HENRY: On the Greeks. And since these students have all been working on your *Antigone,* I'll give them the inside track. They *must*, however—you must tell them this— they *must* let the Dean's office know they're interested, so we'll have some indication of preenrollment.

JUDY: Professor Harper, I'm not sure they'd want to—

HENRY: Oh yes they would. Tell them this course will be— how shall I put it?—"project-oriented." They can put on plays. They can make models of the Parthenon. They can draw maps of the Peloponnesian Peninsula, I don't care!

JUDY: That doesn't sound like you, Professor Harper.

HENRY: Oh yes, yes. And tell them I'll grade it Pass/Fail, if they want. And I'll have very few papers. No papers at all, really, if that's what they want. Because the important thing is not papers, is it, it's the Greeks! We'll be studying the Greeks next year, that's the thing! We'll still be reading and discussing those fine old plays. We'll still be holding onto the heart of Western Civilization. That's what we'll be doing, Miss Miller, and you will have helped us do it! *(Pause)*

JUDY: You mean you want students next year.

HENRY: Yes, frankly, I do. *(Pause)*

JUDY: Wow!

HENRY: There it is.

JUDY: I always thought we had to go through you. I never thought you had to go through *us*.

HENRY: Well we do.

JUDY: You really *need* us, don't you? You have to have us.

HENRY: Without you, we'd die.

JUDY: I never knew that before.

HENRY: Now you do. *(Pause)* So will you tell them about the course?

JUDY: Yes, I will.

HENRY: And you'll encourage them to come?

JUDY: I'll tell them, Professor Harper. I'll let them choose.

HENRY: But you won't . . . undercut me?

JUDY: No, I won't do that.

HENRY: And you'll remind them to sign up immediately. So the administration will know.

JUDY: I'll do all that sir. I mean, you have a right to live, too, after all.

HENRY: You're magnanimous in victory, Miss Miller.

JUDY: Thank you, sir.

HENRY: Now, before we turn to the crass topic of grades, suppose we celebrate the conclusion of these negotiations. *(Opens his drawer again, takes out a sherry bottle and two murky glasses.)* I keep this sherry around for those rare occasions when a fellow scholar stops by.

JUDY: Oh I don't—

HENRY: *(Pouring)* Please. It's important. Old Odysseus and the nymph Calypso, in Book Five of the *Odyssey*, sharing a glass before they say goodbye. *(HE hands her her glass, raises his in a toast.)* To peace and reconciliation. *(They click glasses and drink.)* Doesn't that hit the spot?

JUDY: Actually, it does.

HENRY: Have some more.

JUDY: Oh, well. No. I mean, all right.
(HE *pours her more, and a touch more for himself.* JUDY *gets up.)*
You know, I was just thinking, Professor Harper . . .

HENRY: *(His little joke)* That's always a good sign.

JUDY: No, seriously, I was thinking that you and I are basically very much alike.

HENRY: Ah? And how so?

JUDY: I mean we both see too big a picture.

HENRY: Elucidate, please.

JUDY: Sure. I mean, there you are, always talking about the Greeks versus the Jews, and here I am, talking about the Jews versus all authority.

HENRY: I see.

JUDY: Maybe we should both scale things down.

HENRY: Maybe we should. *(Settling back in his chair)* In any case, I think you can count on receiving a B in my course, Miss Miller.

JUDY: A B.

HENRY: A strong B. A solid B. A B which leans longingly toward a B plus.

JUDY: I was kind of hoping I'd get an A.

HENRY: I don't think your work quite warrants an A, Miss Miller.

JUDY: You don't think so?

HENRY: Let's reserve the A's for Sophocles, shall we? It gives us something to go for. *(Pause)*

JUDY: That's cool.

HENRY: I take it you agree.

JUDY: I guess a B from you is like an A from anyone else.

HENRY: Well, thank you, Miss Miller.

JUDY: *(Getting up)* Besides, I don't really believe in grades anymore.

HENRY: Good for you.

JUDY: I think I've grown beyond them.

HENRY: Unfortunately we live in a world which seems to require them. We have to toss them, like bones, to a ravenous administration.

JUDY: Oh God, I know. *They* even wanted me to take an A.

HENRY: And where did they propose you find that A?

JUDY: A professor in Drama saw a rehearsal, and offered to give me a straight A.

HENRY: Ah, but of course that wouldn't count.

JUDY: Oh sure. He said I could register it under Special Topics.

HENRY: Well then, I'm afraid I'd have to go to the Provost. To protest this blatant interference in my course.

JUDY: I just came from the Provost. It was his idea, actually. *(Pause)*

HENRY: You mean you don't need a grade in my course to graduate.

JUDY: Not any more.

HENRY: You don't really need me at all.

JUDY: Technically, no.

HENRY: Why did you bother to come?

JUDY: I wanted your opinion of my *play*! I wanted to hear what you thought.

HENRY: And I told you: B.

JUDY: Right. Fine. And I'm accepting your B. I'll tell the Registrar.
(SHE *starts out.*)

HENRY: Miss Miller. (SHE *stops.*) This professor who offered to intrude. Who was he?

JUDY: Who?

HENRY: Do I know him?

JUDY: He's new this year.

HENRY: What's his name?

JUDY: Bob Birnbaum.

HENRY: Bob—?

JUDY: Birnbaum. *(Pause)*

HENRY: Of course.

JUDY: What do you mean?

HENRY: Once again Athens is forced to bow to Jersualem.

JUDY: Explain that, please.

HENRY: I mean the Chosen People always choose to intrude.

JUDY: That's what I thought you meant.
(SHE *strides for the door, then wheels on him.*)
All bets are off, Professor Harper. I wouldn't recommend this course to a Nazi! And I'll take a good, solid, Jewish A from Birnbaum!
(SHE *storms out.*)

HENRY: *(Quietly; to himself as he sits)* Good God. What have I done? *(The lights dim on him as he sits at his desk.* DIANA *crosses the stage hurriedly, carrying a stack of folders.* DAVE *is following her.)*

DAVE: Dean . . . ? (SHE *turns*) Could I speak to you for a minute, please?

DIANA: I'm sorry, but I'm late for an important meeting.

DAVE: The Committee on Academic Performance, right?

DIANA: That's the one.

DAVE: That's what I've got to speak to you about. *(SHE stops, looks at him.)*

DIANA: Aren't you that friend of Judy Miller's?

DAVE: David Appleton. My name's coming up before the committee today. I flunked the Chemistry final. I'm not graduating.

DIANA: Chemistry will take care of you. There's infinite salvation: makeup exams, summer school, degrees given out in the fall . . .

DAVE: I don't want any of that. I want to switch to your department and be here all next year.

DIANA: Studying what?

DAVE: The Greeks.

DIANA: But we don't have a Classics Department anymore.

DAVE: You have Professor Harper.

DIANA: He may be on sabbatical next year.

DAVE: Oh. Then I'll make up my general requirements till he returns and take Ancient Greek on my own.

DIANA: *(Starting out)* If you'd make an appointment with Monica, my assistant, we'll discuss all this.

DAVE: No, I've thought it through. I just need your approval.

DIANA: You're talking about another year's tuition.

DAVE: I know. And my dad's cutting me off. But I've gotten a double shift in the cafeteria. I'll get my degree next June, and apply for postgraduate studies with Professor Harper. *(Pause)*

DIANA: I'll tell the committee you're staying on.

DAVE: Thank you.

DIANA: I envy you.

DAVE: For studying with Harper?

DIANA: For being so sure.
(JUDY enters.)

JUDY: What's going on, Dave?

DAVE: I'm changing my life.

DIANA: Make an appointment if you want to change it back!
(SHE goes out.)

JUDY: We have a rehearsal, remember? I'm putting in the final rewrites.

DAVE: Can't make it. Got a class.

JUDY: At this hour? What class?

DAVE: Harper's actually.

DIANA: *Har*per's? *My* Harper?

DAVE: I've been auditing it for the past three weeks.

JUDY: Why?

DAVE: I like him. I like the subject. I like myself when I'm working on it.

JUDY: You never told me that.

DAVE: I knew it would freak you out.

JUDY: Damn right! He's a bigot, Dave.

DAVE: I don't think so.

JUDY: He's an anti-Semite.

DAVE: I don't think so, Judy.

JUDY: I *know* so! *Personally!* He made an anti-Semitic *slur!*

DAVE: He just generalizes, Judy. It's his tragic flaw.

JUDY: I don't buy that, Dave.

DAVE: All right, so he made a crack. So what? People make ethnic digs all the time in this country. We all get it in the neck—the Poles, the Italians, now the Wasps.

JUDY: The Jews are different! All through history—

DAVE: So I keep hearing. Still, seems to me you're people, like everyone else. I think this Jewish thing is getting out of hand. Suddenly nothing counts except you're Jewish!

JUDY: Dave . . .

DAVE: No, let me finish, for once in my life! I didn't fall in love with a Jewish Revolutionary. I fell in love with *you!* I fell in love with a particular person who liked Springsteen and moo shoo pork and staying in bed all day on Sunday. What happened to all that? What happens to us next *year?* These are the important things—not that you're Jewish, for God's sake!

JUDY: I think we're in a little hot water here.

DAVE: I guess we are. *(A bell rings).* Saved by the bell. (HE *starts off.)*

JUDY: Dave. (HE *stops.)* We have rehearsal now.

DAVE: Work around me.

JUDY: It's too late for that.

DAVE: Look, it's his last class. The whole school knows about this. Everyone wants to see what he's going to say.

JUDY: Not if they're with *Antigone.*

DAVE: Give me an hour.

JUDY: No! It's him or me, Dave. You choose.

DAVE: Be serious.

JUDY: I am. I'll put in Mark Shapiro. I'll replace you. Totally. *(Pause)*

DAVE: Fair enough.
(HE *starts off again.*)

JUDY: *(Calling after him)* Then it's true, what my grandmother said! You people always turn your backs when
the chips are down! (HE *turns, glares at her, then exits.*
SHE *speaks softly, to herself.*) Oh Lord, I'm as bad as
Harper.
(SHE *goes off slowly the opposite way. The lights come up
on* HENRY *as he comes D., addressing the audience once
again as if it were his class.* DAVE *enters, to sit on the side
and listen, as if he were in class.*)

HENRY: *(To audience)* This has been a course on tragedy.
That is what this course is supposed to be about. *(Pause)*
First, let me remind you what tragedy is *not*. Tragedy
has nothing to do with choice. If you can choose, it is not
tragic. There are some people who think that our arms
race with the Russians is tragic. It is not. It is not,
because we have the choice, they have the choice, to say
No, to stop, to disarm, to embrace each other in the
name of peace at any time. So it is not tragic. It is stupid,
yes. It is insane, it is suicidal, it is pathetic, but it is
not—repeat Not—tragic, in the true Greek sense of the
word. *(Pause)* Tragedy occurs when you cannot choose,
when you have no choice at all. This is hard for Americans to understand. Because most of us are free, or think
we are. Nowhere else in the world, and never before in
history, have so many people been so free to choose so
many destinies. Perhaps, because of this freedom, it is
impossible for us to sense what the Greeks called tragedy. We have no oracles, no gods, no real sense of
ultimate authority to insist that if we do one thing, another will inevitably follow. We are free. *(Pause)* On the
other hand, there might come a time to some of us, to
one or two, (HE *glances at Dave.*) when we get an in-
kling, a glimmer, a faint shadow of a shadow of what it
might have been like for the Greeks when they sat in a
theater and saw the universe close in on a man, or
woman, because of some flaw, some excess, some over-

shooting of the mark . . . *(Pause)* Then the net tightens, and as he struggles, tightens further, until he is crushed by forces total and absurd. *(Pause)* Then we might be touching the outer borders of tragedy, as the Greeks once knew it. *(Pause.* HE *takes up his book of* Antigone.*)* But I've just discovered something else about tragedy, or at least about Sophoclean tragedy. Something I thought I knew, but didn't understand till now. And that is what the tragic heroes do after the net has closed around them. What they do, even in the teeth of disaster, is accept responsibility, assert their own destiny, and mete out proudly their own punishments. This is what Oedipus does when he puts out his eyes. This is what Antigone does, when she hangs herself. And this is what Creon does, at the end of the same play. He has lost his wife, his children, all he holds dear. And he realizes why: that in his commitment to abstract and dehumanizing laws, he has neglected the very heart of life. And so he banishes himself from his own city. His Polis. He goes. He disappears. He leaves the stage, forever doomed now to wander far from the only community he knows, self-exiled and alone. *(Pause)* I'll expect all papers under my door by five o'clock this evening. You may retrieve them, graded and with appropriate comments, from the departmental office next Monday. Enjoy your summer. Read good books. Go to good plays. Think of the Greeks. Thank you and goodbye.

*(*HE *sees* DAVE *go, then crosses to his desk, where he leaves his book of* Antigone. *Then* HE *exits, as graduation music comes up loudly: an optimistic piece, played by a brass ensemble.* DIANA *comes out in gown and colorful academic hood.* SHE *reads from a formal-looking document.)*

DIANA: Our final award is the Peabody Prize . . . *(Reads from card)* "Offered annually to that student who best combines academic excellence with extracurricular commitment . . ." *(To audience)* It is awarded this year to Judith Rachel Miller, of the graduating class, for her exceptional academic record as well as for her fascinating contemporary version of Sophocles' *Antigone. (Applause and cheers.* JUDY *comes on, in academic robes.* SHE *accepts an envelope from* DIANA, *who gives her a kiss.)* Congratulations, Judy . . . And now refreshments will be—

JUDY: May I say something, please?

DIANA: *(Very reluctantly)* All right.

JUDY: *(To audience)* First, I want to thank everyone involved for making our play possible. *(Looks at envelope)* And I want to thank the Peabody Foundation for making this prize possible. *(Looks out)* And I want to thank my parents for making *me* possible. (DIANA *tries to step in.)* I'm not finished. (DIANA *steps back. To audience.)* Lately I've been doing some thinking, and as someone once told me, that's always a good sign. I've been thinking about this prize, for example. I guess it stands for everything I used to believe in: personal ambition . . . success . . . (SHE *peeks into the envelope.)* And sure, why not? money . . . I mean, these are the things they tell us make our country great . . . (DIANA *looks worried.)* Trouble is, I'm beginning to think these things aren't so important. Maybe my play hasn't influenced anyone else, but it sure has influenced me. I don't feel good about my life anymore. I don't feel good about my country. I can't accept all this *stuff* that's going on these days. I can't accept it. No, I'm sorry, but I just can't accept it.
(SHE *hands the envelope back to* DIANA *and hurries off.)*

DIANA: Judy!
(SHE *hurries off after* JUDY, *as the lights come up on* HENRY's *office.* DAVE *enters, carrying a note. He finds* HENRY's *book on the desk. He picks it up, looks at it, and started deciphering the title.)*

DAVE: Alpha . . . Nu . . . Tau . . . Iota . . . Gamma . . . Omicron . . . Nu . . . Eta . . . *Antigone* . . . (DIANA *enters, no longer in her robes, but still carrying the prize envelope.)*

DIANA: Mr. Appleton? Monica told me you got a note from Professor Harper.

DAVE: *(Indicating the book)* He said he was leaving me his book.

DIANA: But did he say where he'd *be?* We can't locate him anywhere.

DAVE: He just mentions the book.

DIANA: Oh dear.

DAVE: I'll find him. I'll track him down. Like Telemachus. In the *Odyssey.*

DIANA: You're beginning to sound a little like him.

DAVE: Maybe. In some ways.

DIANA: I suppose you heard about Judy.

DAVE: Saw it. From the sidelines.

DIANA: That girl seems to be interested in systematically hanging herself.

DAVE: She likes to go for broke.

DIANA: This prize is a sizable check. Do you know any cause she'd want to donate it to?

DAVE: Tell you what: I'll ask her. It'll give me an excuse to open diplomatic relations.

DIANA: I have a feeling we may have lost them both forever.

DAVE: Oh God, I hope not.

DIANA: So do I . . . Meanwhile, I have no idea how to summarize all this for the departmental report. What does Sophocles say at the end of that damn play?

DAVE: Well, he says that wisdom and reverence lead to happiness . . .

DIANA: Oh good. I'll go along with that! Thank you.
(DAVE *starts out, then stops, turns back.)*

DAVE: But then he goes on to say that we only learn this when we're too old for it to make much difference.

DIANA: Then heaven help us all. *(They look at each other. Blackout.)*

THE END

THE PERFECT PARTY

A Comedy in Two Acts

The Perfect Party was first produced in the Studio Theatre of Playwrights Horizons in New York City on April
2, 1986. It was directed by John Tillinger; the set was
designed by Steven Rubin; the costumes were by Jane
Greenwood; the lighting was by Dan Kotlowitz; and the
production stage manager was Suzanne Fry. The cast
was as follows:

TONY	John Cunningham
LOIS	Charlotte Moore
SALLY	Debra Mooney
WES	David Margulies
WILMA	Kate McGregor-Stewart

The Perfect Party moved to the Astor Place Theatre in New York City on June 24, 1986, under the auspices of Nicholas Benton, Stanley Flink, Norma and David Langworthy, Craig MacDonald, and Nathan Weiss. The cast was as follows:

TONY	John Cunningham
LOIS	Charlotte Moore
SALLY	Debra Mooney
WES	Stephen Pearlman
WILMA	June Gable

To André Bishop

CAST

TONY   a middle-aged college professor
SALLY   his wife
LOIS   a reporter
WES   Tony's friend
WILMA   Wes's wife

The play takes place in Tony's study, somewhat set apart from the rest of his house. It is a comfortable room, possibly wood-paneled, with a desk, a couch, several chairs, plenty of books in bookcases, and good prints on the wall. Among these might be a picture of Monticello, a portrait of Hawthorne, a profile of Fitzgerald. There is also a television cabinet, possibly a stereo, and a VCR. One door upstage opens onto a hallway leading to the rest of the downstairs area.

ACT I

AT RISE: Tony *and* Lois *enter from the hall. Tony is a good-looking, middle-aged man, dressed in a tuxedo. Lois is also good-looking and wears an elegant black dress.*

LOIS: I understand you plan to make this a perfect party.

TONY: I certainly plan to try.
(HE goes to a bar, which has been set up on top of his desk, and begins pouring her a Perrier.)

LOIS: No, no. I'm serious. You announced it as such. You sent out invitations. I brought mine along.
(SHE produces an elegant invitation from her purse. It might be decorated with the logo from the program.)
"Come," you say here, "to a perfect party."

TONY: Did I write that?

LOIS: I believe you did. Unless someone is sending out invitations under your name.

TONY: No, no. I'll admit it. I wrote it. It's just that hearing it read aloud, on the eve of battle, so to speak, makes me a little nervous.

LOIS: I should imagine.

TONY: Washington before Yorktown.

LOIS: Yes.

TONY: Custer, before the Little Big Horn.

LOIS: Now, now.

185

TONY: Well, there are bound to be doubts.

LOIS: But you're still committed, aren't you? You still plan to give it a go?

TONY: Oh yes. Absolutely. All the way.

LOIS: Good. Otherwise I'm wasting my time. And possibly yours.
(HE *brings her her drink.*)

TONY: Are you sure you won't have something stronger than Perrier?

LOIS: No, no. I have to keep a clear head. I have to decide whether to write you up.

TONY: I see.

LOIS: Besides, I happen to represent a major New York newspaper. It would be against the very grain of my profession if I drank on the job.

TONY: I understand.

LOIS: You, of course, should feel free to indulge.

TONY: I thought I might.

LOIS: After all, you must feel very much on the line. I mean, a perfect party.

TONY: At least I can start with a perfect martini.
(HE *returns to the bar to mix his own drink.*)

LOIS: A martini? That takes considerable courage.

TONY: I'm hoping it will give me considerably more.

LOIS: I notice you've made the party Black Tie.

TONY: Well I think people look and act their best in evening clothes.

LOIS: I tend to agree. Possibly because I'm a naturalist at heart—with a special fondness for the panda and the penguin.

TONY: Ah.

LOIS: *(Walking around)* I want to know about this room.

TONY: This is my study.

LOIS: That tells me very little.

TONY: Ah, well, then I'll tell you more. When my wife and I first bought this house, we called this room the den, possibly because we'd hibernate in here after dinner, like two contented bears, to engage in post-prandial love-play. Naturally, children arrived, and this became known as the family room. Our several cubs would barge in here at all times of the day or night, spilling food, tripping over toys, to gather around the cold, unblinking eye of what I call the Cyclops.
(HE *opens a cabinet, displays a television screen, closes it deftly.)*
Finally, when my wife went to work, and my children left home, I moved my books in here, and turned it totally into my study.

LOIS: *(Sitting on the couch, taking notes from time to time.)* All that says a great deal about American marriage, and the diminishing role of the male within it.

TONY: I may be diminished, but I'm still indispensable. Here's where I pay a good part of the bills. And here's where I prepare courses on American history and literature, which I teach at a local university.

LOIS: Hence your earlier references to American battles.

TONY: Exactly. *(Indicates books in bookcase.)*
And these are some of the authors I teach: Hawthorne, James, Fitzgerald, Cheever, Updike . . .

LOIS: Of course. I've already noticed some of their themes and rhythms, even in your casual discourse.

TONY: Yes, but I have other strings to my bow. Note over here I also have the complete works of Oscar Wilde, bound in leather.

LOIS: Oscar Wilde?

TONY: I inherited him from my grandmother.

LOIS: The source is immaterial. I'd be careful of Wilde. He's not American, and tends to undermine everything that is.

TONY: Nonetheless, here's where I keep him. And here's where we can talk, without being disturbed by the preparations for this evening's party which are taking place, as it were, offstage.

LOIS: And I suppose here's where you wrote the invitations.

TONY: That's right.

LOIS: Including the one which found its way to my newspaper.

TONY: Yes.

LOIS: Did you send it yourself, or did some public relations person slip it into the mail?

TONY: I sent it myself.

LOIS: May I ask why?

TONY: I thought it was news.

LOIS: That, of course, depends on what you tell me. For example, what gave you the idea for this party, and what do you hope to achieve by giving it? Remember while you're talking that I come from New York, which is a hectic, fast-paced city and makes us easily bored with unnecessary exposition.

TONY: A perfect party. Well. I think everyone in the world secretly wants to give one. It's at the heart of the social impulse. The caveman calling his fellow tribesman to the fire, the astrophysicist cupping his electronic ear to space—we all have this yearning to connect in some ultimate way with our fellow man.

LOIS: Or woman?

TONY: Of course. Sorry.

LOIS: Then would you define a perfect party?

TONY: A perfect party has a perfect shape. It starts, it builds, it crests, it explodes, and when it finally subsides, everyone involved—he who gives it, she who attends—is bathed in the pleasant afterglow of sweet remembrance.

LOIS: You make it sound vaguely sexual.

TONY: Do I? I hope I don't offend.

LOIS: No, no. I like sex, coming as I do from New York. But now I must ask you what we call colloquially the Passover question: namely, why now? Why is this night different from all other nights?

TONY: Well, I'm not getting any younger. I hear the clock ticking away. I've lived a complicated life in a complicated country, and I feel the compulsion to pull it all together in some sort of pattern, some sort of shape, just once, at least for an evening, before I die.

LOIS: Hmm. That's very touching . . . You're a persuasive man. Persuasive and charming . . . Much of what you say has a strange appeal. Sometimes I have the feeling that you're slightly naive, but that could simply come from the fact that you don't live in New York. Occasionally, also, you seem a little ornate, but I put that down to the unnecessary influence of Oscar Wilde.

TONY: So will you write me up?

LOIS: That now depends on your guest list.

TONY: Ah. Well. I happen to have one right here.
(HE *produces a lovely, elegantly tooled leather folder.*)

LOIS: *(Taking it.)* What a charming way to display your guests. I almost said perfect, but I didn't.
(SHE *opens it.*)
And what helpful headings. School chums. College pals. Navy buddies. Academic colleagues. *(To Tony)* There's an awful lot of male bonding going on here, sir.

TONY: Read on. The women come in later with a vengeance.

LOIS: *(Reading)* Old girls. Young students. Recreational companions. Sexual partners. Couldn't some of these categories be combined?

TONY: Good idea.

LOIS: *(Reading on)* Family members . . . I'm glad to see you've squeezed your family in here somewhere.

TONY: They're an important part of my life.

LOIS: I always worry about those poor old mothers, sitting alone in the corner with their knees apart.

TONY: My mother keeps her knees together.

LOIS: I'm glad to hear it. *(She returns to the folder.)* Let's see what else. "Miscellaneous"? What's this "miscellaneous"?

TONY: Oh those are just people who don't fall into any particular category. People I've met and clicked with over the years. For example, there's a waiter from Buffalo, New York.

LOIS: How sweet. Which reminds me: did you get a chance to do any kind of ethnic or demographic breakdown on this guest list?

TONY: Well I avoided quotas. I don't believe in those. But I can say that I tried to include a full spectrum of racial and regional diversity. There are also several people coming whose sexual orientation is hardly conventional, and I've asked a smattering of mentally and physically handicapped. I've also taken the liberty of inviting two registered Republicans, just to leaven the lump.

LOIS: *(Closing the folder)* I'm impressed.

TONY: Thank you.

LOIS: Extremely impressed.

TONY: Thank you very much.

LOIS: *(Patting the folder)* What you've got here seems to be a kind of microcosm for America itself, in the waning years of the twentieth century.

TONY: Exactly.

LOIS: So if it works, if the party succeeds, it will mean that America itself, as a social and political experiment, will have succeeded.

TONY: That's it.

LOIS: So you and I are not just sitting around talking about a party, are we? There's a good deal more at stake tonight than that. What we're talking about, really, is whether this nation, or any other nation so constituted, can long endure.

TONY: Right!

LOIS: *(Getting up; enthusiastically)* Goddamnit, I'm going to put that in the paper, if I can improve the phrasing.

TONY: That must mean you've decided to write me up.

LOIS: I've decided more than that. I've decided to review you.

TONY: Review me? Do you mean that?

LOIS: Absolutely. Tomorrow morning, your party will receive a full-length review, possibly with a picture, in a major New York newspaper!

TONY: Fantastic! That's what I was hoping for.

LOIS: Well first, of course, I had to size you up.

TONY: I was terrified you might just settle for an announcement. Like a wedding. Or a funeral.

LOIS: No, no. We are running for the roses now.
(SHE *folds up her notebook and tosses it down on the coffee table.)*
I'm not even going to take any more notes. That might be distracting to you and to your guests. From here on

in, I'm simply going to sit back and judge, coolly and dispassionately, with the interests of several million readers at heart.
(Pause.)

TONY: I wish you'd let me spike that Perrier with a little splash of white wine.

LOIS: I've already told you, sir: there are ethics in my profession which make that an immediate no-no.

TONY: At least call me Tony.

LOIS: I'm not even sure I should do that.

TONY: Oh come on. This is a party.

LOIS: All right, then. Tony.

TONY: And I may call you . . . what?

LOIS: Lois.

TONY: Lois. A lovely name, Lois.

LOIS: You may compliment my name, Tony, you may tempt me with alcohol, but I assure you right now I cannot be bought.

TONY: I see.
(LOIS looks at her watch.)

LOIS: Now we've only a little more time before your guests arrive. I want to tell you something important. Something which probably no critic has ever before told the person about to be criticized.

TONY: Go on.

LOIS: When your invitation announcing a perfect party came across my desk at Arts and Leisure, something happened to me. I mean, *physically*. The hair on the back of my neck stood up, and my whole body began to shake violently.

TONY: Why, Lois?

LOIS: Because I suddenly thought: here might be the chance to write a perfect review!

TONY: Ah.

LOIS: Immediately, I ran into my editor's office. I pounded his desk, like some sob sister out of an old movie. I said, "Look, buster! Here's some guy out in the provinces planning a perfect party! Lemme at him!"

TONY: And he did.

LOIS: He did and he didn't. He said he'd print the review if it were any good. But I had to write it on spec. And I had to pay my own transportation here and back. For economic reasons, I took Peoples Express.

TONY: I appreciate the sacrifice.

LOIS: It was worth it. To get here. Because after I write this review, and see it printed, and hear it celebrated in the world at large, as God is my witness, I'll never fly Peoples again!

TONY: You're an ambitious woman, Lois.

LOIS: I am, Tony, but so are you. We are both onto something big tonight. Here you are, about to recreate the multiplicity of America under your own roof. And here I am, about to review that attempt for a major New York newspaper. Oh look, my friend, we were born to meet, you and I. We are dependent on each other. We are locked together in a profound embrace, like Ahab and the whale.

TONY: Couldn't you just relax and enjoy the evening?

LOIS: I could not. If I did, people would be giving parties from here to Hawaii, and calling them perfect, when they might not be at all.

TONY: But what's wrong with that?

LOIS: There have to be standards in this world, Tony, and naturally, I'd like to be the one who sets them.

TONY: Oh God, that means we've got to be perfectly wonderful tonight, don't we?

LOIS: That, or perfectly terrible. Either way, it will make for a perfect review. *(There is a knocking on the door.)* Meanwhile, someone wants to come in, and frankly I'm rather glad, since our rhetoric was becoming a little inflated.

TONY: *(Calling toward door)* Come in.
(The door opens. SALLY *enters in a lovely evening dress, carrying a tray of hors d'oeuvres.)*

SALLY: I was getting bored hanging around in the hall, fussing with flowers, coping with caterers.

TONY: *(Going to greet her)* Enter my wife Sally, powdered and perfumed from her bath! Gosh, Sally, you look just about as lovely as a woman of your age and general configuration can possibly look. *(He kisses her.)* Darling, this is Lois, who has come all the way from New York to check us out, and write us up.

SALLY: And possibly to put us down, am I right, Lois?

LOIS: Not unless you hurt, confuse, or bore me, Sally. *(They shake hands.)*

SALLY: I'll try to do none of those things. I do hope, however, that somewhere along the line, I'll get a chance to express my true feelings.

TONY: Uh-oh.

LOIS: Your true *feelings*? Do you mean to say, Sally, that your true feelings are not in tune with this party, and you are actually, in this day and age, trying to cover them *up*?

SALLY: I'll say no more, though you'll notice how difficult it is for me to maintain eye contact.

TONY: Uh-oh.

LOIS: *(Looking from one to the other)* It's against both my personal and professional ethics to intervene between a husband and wife. *(Pause)* Unless I sense a story. I sense one now. How do you feel about this party, Sally? Be frank.

SALLY: *(Passing the hors d'oeuvres)* I feel this is a perfect party, and we are perfectly in accord. Have some hors d'oeuvres.

LOIS: I still sense trouble at the top of the evening. It may well affect my reviews.

TONY: *(Quickly)* The party wouldn't be perfect, Sally, if you didn't feel free to express an opinion.

SALLY: Then I don't like it very much.

TONY: Sally, my love—

SALLY: In fact I hate it. I hate the salmon mousse they're preparing in the kitchen. I hate the Chivas Regal being set up in the hall. I hate this goddamn dress which I bought on sale, at Lord and Taylor, out at that stupid, boring, fucking Mall!

TONY: It's a beautiful dress, Sally, and you look lovely in it.

SALLY: It stinks. It sucks. I hate it. You could feed a number of hungry people with what I paid for it. You could buy a respectable portion of a cat-scanner. You could reclaim several acres of wetlands with what I coughed up for this goddamn dress.

TONY: Civilization is expensive, Sally. I've told you that on a number of occasions.

SALLY: Then civilization is horseshit, if this is what it leads to.

TONY: Gosh, Sally. Wow. Gee whiz. I have to say I wasn't quite prepared for such strong feelings. Upstairs, in our bedroom, when you were putting on your earrings, I do remember hearing vague mutterings of discontent. But I didn't expect this explosion of distaste. It startles me, darling. And puzzles me as well.

LOIS: Perhaps I'm to blame here. I've known people to exaggerate their performances in front of critics. Maybe I'll go and review the mousse. (SHE *starts to leave.*)

TONY: No, no. Please.

SALLY: Yes. Please stay. You give me a vague sense of sisterhood at a time when I need it most.

TONY: It couldn't be a perfect party, Lois, if you only reviewed the food.

SALLY: Shit! There's that expression again. "A perfect party!" What if it isn't perfect, Tony? What if two of your buddy-pals get into a boring argument about batting averages? What if someone spills a drink, or loses his teeth, or puts a cigarette out in a dessert plate?

LOIS: What if someone even *smokes*, for that matter?

SALLY: *Exactly*, Lois. Or what if someone, totally accidentally, farts?

TONY: Good Lord.

SALLY: What if that happens? Does that mean the party is no longer perfect, Tony? Does Lois here go back to New York and tell the world we produced a disaster?

LOIS: Oh well, let's cross that bridge when we come to it.

TONY: I'm sure that Lois will leave some margin for error.

LOIS: Not really. I might if I were from Boston or Saint Louis, but since I'm from New York, I'm compelled to be brutal.

SALLY: *(To* TONY*)* You see? We're setting ourselves up here! I may not be a la-de-da college professor, but I know hubris when I see it. When people start wandering around the house talking about perfect parties, and inviting New York newspapers to write them up, then I get a primitive Sophoclean shudder. We are challenging the gods here tonight, Tony, and I don't like it one iota!

TONY: *(To* LOIS*)* Sally majored in Classy Civ at Vassar.

SALLY: Yes, but I got my master's in social responsibility at a community college.

TONY: Have a drink, Sally.

SALLY: I don't want a drink.

LOIS: He's always trying to persuade people to have drinks.

TONY: I'm simply trying to be a good host.

SALLY: Or else you're trying to drown a serious disagreement in a pool of alcohol.

TONY: I like to think—

SALLY: All *right*, Tony! I will have a *drink*. I've decided to have . . . *(She thinks.)* . . . a Box Car.

TONY: A—Box Car?

SALLY: It's a drink which emerged during the Depression.

TONY: I'm not sure I know what's in a Box Car.

SALLY: You don't? And you're a perfect host?

TONY: I'm not sure I have the ingredients immediately available.

SALLY: *(Casually)* Oh well, then, this isn't a perfect party.

TONY: *(Grimly)* I'll make you a Box Car, Sally. There's a copy of *The Joy of Cooking* in the kitchen, and it has a complete section devoted to exotic beverages. I'll make you a Box Car, Sally, and you can be damn sure it will be a perfect one! *(*HE *goes out, slamming the door. Pause.)*

SALLY: *(To* LOIS*)* That was a ploy.

LOIS: I figured as much.

SALLY: To get him out of the room.

LOIS: Yes, I picked up on that.

SALLY: I don't really want a Box Car at all. *(Gets up and goes to the bar.)* What I really want is a tad of white wine, and I hope you'll join me, Lois.

LOIS: I shouldn't. But since you're a woman, I will.

SALLY: *(At bar)* Then you agree with what I said about a sense of sisterhood, Lois.

LOIS: I certainly do. I resonated as soon as you walked in this room.

SALLY: I've simply got to talk to someone of the same sex about what I've been going through, recently, on this perfect party business.

LOIS: Feel free to talk. I'll consider it strictly off the record. If I write it up, I'll attribute it to unnamed sources.

SALLY: *(Bringing down the drinks)* Well it's been hell, frankly. That man has become obsessed with parties, particularly perfect ones.

LOIS: He certainly seems to have an idée fixe, doesn't he?

SALLY: It's appalling. Ever since the children began leaving home, it's as if he were trying to reconstitute the family. On a large and general scale. With himself once again in control.

LOIS: How awful. You must feel as if you're living right in the middle of a bad translation of Molière.

SALLY: I do. It pervades our life. Whenever we go out, whenever we have people in, he has these huge expectations that the evening will click into place like some smooth, well-oiled machine. When it doesn't happen— and of course it doesn't—he is profoundly disappointed. He sits on the edge of the bed, in his pajamas, holding his head and groaning.

LOIS: When he should be making love to you.

SALLY: Exactly! Oh it's a mess, Lois. Our marriage is teetering on the brink.

LOIS: Now, now. Think positively.

SALLY: I'm trying to, Lois. But there's so much at stake here. Do you realize that he's quit his job because of this party.

LOIS: What?

SALLY: He has quit his job. He had a perfectly good job teaching American studies at a reputable university. The salary was insulting, but the fringe benefits made up for it.

LOIS: Did he have tenure?

SALLY: He most certainly did. And he was considered an excellent teacher. At least until recently.

LOIS: What happened recently?

SALLY: He tried to turn every class into a perfect class. The students rebelled, of course, and switched into Abnormal Psychology. That's when he quit, so he could turn his total attention to this party.

LOIS: But how does he expect to live, when the party's over?

SALLY: He expects to become a consultant.

LOIS: A consultant?

SALLY: On parties! That's why he brought you into the picture. He desperately wants a review. Because he desperately wants to become a celebrity.

LOIS: But that's what *I* want to be! And there's only room for a few of us at the top!

SALLY· I can't help it. That's what he wants. He says he comes from what was once the ruling class and if he can no longer lead this nation toward a more perfect union, he can at least show it how to entertain!

LOIS: Yes, but a consultant!

SALLY: I know. He sees himself travelling around the country giving lectures and seminars and workshops on parties in America, and how to give them. The other night he dreamed he was on the *Merv Griffin Show*.

LOIS: Oh no.

SALLY: That's what he dreamed.

LOIS: But that's outrageous! Merv is very choosy about his guests.

SALLY: You know that, I know that, Merv knows that, but Tony doesn't know it. He even thinks he might host a show of his own some day. On nationwide TV.

LOIS: No.

SALLY: Or at least co-host.

LOIS: I'm stunned.

SALLY: I'm telling you, the man is obsessed. Did he show you his guest list?

LOIS: Yes he did, and I must say it was impressively democratic.

SALLY: I'm talking about his secret guest list.

LOIS: His *secret* guest list?

SALLY: He has a secret list of people whom he's asked to this party, and who he hopes will suddenly show up.

LOIS: Who's on it?

SALLY: Oh, God. Let me think. Abba Eban's on it.

LOIS: Abba Eban?

SALLY: Abba Eban is on that list. He thinks Abba Eban would be an addition to any party.

LOIS: Well, of course he would be, but . . .

SALLY: Ginger Rogers is also on the list.

LOIS: Ginger's on it?

SALLY: Absolutely. He's even bought a record of old dance tunes. If she shows up, he plans to roll back the rug, and spin her around the floor, to the tune of *Follow the Fleet.*

LOIS: That is sheer . . .

SALLY: Hubris is the word. I've already used it.

LOIS: You poor soul. Living with that.

SALLY: I'm all right. Think of him. Living constantly in the gap between how he wishes people would behave, and how they actually do. And trying to bridge that gap with this party, this evening.

LOIS: Sally: I can't tell you how much I appreciate your telling me these things. Women do connect in ways which are far beyond the world of men. I think we've proved that in the discussion we've had just now.

SALLY: Then I wonder if I might ask you a small favor.

LOIS: Name it.

SALLY: Give him a good review.

LOIS: What?

SALLY: Oh I'm not talking about a rave. You don't have to do that. Just compliment him on the basic idea. Mention a few good moments. Give him enough quotes so that he can show his clippings around.

LOIS: I can't do that, Sally.

SALLY: Of course you can.

LOIS: Sally, I can't. If I did that, if I let my affection for you influence my response, it would open the door to the most shoddy enterprises.

SALLY: But his future depends on what you say here.

LOIS: So does mine, dear heart. Don't think for one minute I'm not on the line here, too. My editor has his eye on this one. If I'm good, then he might promote me to White House functions and Hollywood galas. But if I fake it, if I strike one false note, then I might find myself a permanent stringer, doomed to cover church suppers and bowling tournaments in areas beyond even a commuting distance from New York.

SALLY: But think about Tony and me.

LOIS: Excuse me, Sally, but these days I find it hard to think about anyone but myself. We live in a narcissistic age, and it's foolish not to take advantage of it.

SALLY: But if you pan us, what will we do financially with Tony out of a job? We've got a kid still in college, and our VCR needs serious repairing.

LOIS: I can't help that, Sally. I've said all along that I must call this evening as I see it, and the Devil take the hindmost, even if the hindmost is your husband.

SALLY: *(Grimly)* Then there's only one thing left for me to do.

LOIS: What's that?

SALLY: I'm not sure, but I'm hoping it will occur to me any minute. (TONY *enters, carrying a strange looking, dark brown drink, garnished with a limp radish, on a silver tray.)*

TONY: One Box Car, coming up. *(*HE *hands it to* SALLY.*)*

SALLY: *(Eying it)* What's in it?

TONY: I doubt if you'd want to know. Let me simply say that, like this evening, I hope the whole is greater than the sum of its parts. (SALLY *looks at it, sips it.)* As for you, Lois, I'm delighted to see you with a wine glass in your hand. It indicates that you're taking a more participatory position.

LOIS: *(Wryly)* Not at all. This happens to be a cool, dry, disengaged Chablis, with a slightly skeptical bouquet.

SALLY: *(Suddenly putting down her glass)* Uh-oh.

TONY: What?

SALLY: This drink.

TONY: What about it?

SALLY: It doesn't agree with me at all. You'll have to call off the party.

TONY: Oh no.

SALLY: I'm serious. I feel perfectly awful. I've got a headache, and heartburn, and a mild case of psoriasis.

TONY: *(Going to her)* Darling . . .

SALLY: *(Getting up)* No, it's getting worse. Don't touch me. I've got to go right to bed. Here's what you better do. Post a sign on the door, saying that the party's cancelled. Pay off the caterers, and get a reasonable rakeoff for what we didn't consume. Call Lois a cab. Tell the university you were just teasing when you quit. Then scramble some eggs, and bring them up to me on a tray, and maybe I'll feel well enough to sit up and have a nice game of Trivial Pursuit. Go on, honey. Get started. (SHE *is almost out the door.)*

TONY: Sally.

SALLY: What, for God's sake?

TONY: I don't believe you're sick at all.

SALLY: What do you mean? I'm about to upchuck all over the door.

TONY: I don't believe that, Sally. And I don't think Lois believes it.

LOIS: I most certainly do not.

SALLY: *(Whirling on* Lois*)* Some sisterhood.

LOIS: I'm sorry, Sally. It's an implausible development, and I'd have to review it as such.

SALLY: Couldn't we all just go to the movies, or something?

LOIS: The movies are out of my bailiwick, Sally. Somebody else is assigned to review those.

SALLY: So I'm caught, aren't I?

TONY: I'm afraid you are, love.

SALLY: There's a moment in the *Iliad* . . .

TONY: *(Quickly; to* Lois*)* Sally was cum laude at Vassar . . .

SALLY: There's a moment in the *Iliad* when Andromache joins Hector on the walls of Troy, right before he goes to his death at the hands of the Greeks. She says she hates what he's about to do, but she'll stand by him to the end while he does it. (SHE *takes Tony's arm and defiantly faces* LOIS.*)* This reminds me of that moment.

LOIS: I appreciate your loyalty, though I question your analogy. *(A door bell rings, far Offstage.)*
But that must be your first guests, thank God. Much as I like you both, I'm interested in seeing a few new faces.

TONY: *(Looking at his watch)* It's still a little early for guests. Unless it's the Murchisons, who always arrive early and eat up all the Brie.

SALLY: I told the Murchisons to be late, for exactly that reason.
(The Offstage door bell rings again.)

LOIS: Maybe you should answer the door.

TONY: Since I'm paying a catering company a great deal of money to do exactly that, I'm hoping I won't have to.

LOIS: I like the suspense. I find it charming.
*(*SHE *sits down).*

TONY: *(Quickly) I* know who it is! It's our great friends, Wes and Wilma Wellman, who live down the street. They've realized the importance of the occasion, and have come over early to help us out.

SALLY: Exactly. Whenever we've been in a crisis situation— when my grandmother died or the dishwasher broke down—the Wellmans rushed right over to be by our side.

(The door bell rings once again.)

TONY: *(Opening the study door)* Yes. Now I hear their gentle voices murmuring in the front hall.

WILMA'S VOICE: *(From Offstage, loudly)* Yoo hoo!

TONY: *(Calling out)* In the study, friends! *(To* LOIS*)* What is a party without true friends at your side? And what better friends could a man have than this stalwart and attractive couple? *(*HE *looks out down the hall.)* Good gravy, it's Wes and Wilma, all right, but I'm not sure they're dressed for the occasion. *(*WES *and* WILMA *enter awkwardly in old bathrobes. Wilma wears a bandana around her hair.)*

SALLY: You do look a little informal, dear friends.

WES: *(Anxiously)* Tony, old pal, we had to rush over and tell you immediately.

TONY: Tell me what, old friends?

WILMA: We can't come to your party.

TONY: Can't come?

WES: Can't come.

TONY: But you answered affirmatively. I put your names in the yes column. I gave the count to the caterer.

WILMA: Things have come up, Tony.

WES: Personal things. Talk to you later. *(*HE *grabs* WILMA *and starts out.)*

TONY: Wait, wait, wait! At least say hello to Lois.

WES: Hello, Lois.

WILMA: Hello, Lois.

LOIS: Hello, Wes and Wilma.

WILMA: *(Taking* WES*'s arm)* Come on, Wes.

WES: *(Staring at* LOIS*)* Hold it. I know this woman from somewhere.

LOIS: I've slept with a number of men, but I don't think you were one of them.

WES: *(Moving toward her)* No, this was prior to puberty . . . (HE *thinks.)* Kindergarten, *(*HE *remembers.)* P.S. 101. Brooklyn.

LOIS: You seem to have touched on my educational beginnings, though I like to think I've grown beyond them.

TONY: *(Hastily)* I'm sure you have, Lois.

WES: You were a strange little girl. You sent out bitter, vindictive Valentines to the whole class. And when it came time for the school play—the Teddy Bear's Picnic, I think it was—you sat on the sidelines and loudly complained about the lighting.

TONY: Lois is a critic, Wes. How good to hear that her talents emerged at such an early age.

WILMA: I'm finding it difficult to contribute to the conversation, because I went to private school in the suburbs of Cleveland.

TONY: That's all right, Wilma. Lois is here from New York to write up the party.

LOIS: I am indeed. And I'm already impatient with these sentimental reminiscences. What we were, or did, when we were young is of interest only to our parents and our psychiatrists. What interests *me* is why you two have arrived embarrassingly early and strangely underdressed. This is the time when most people are still in the shower or poking around in their clothes closets, deciding what to wear and who to be.

WES: That's exactly where we were, five minutes ago.

LOIS: In the shower? Or in the closet?

WILMA: *(Taking* WES*'s arm)* In the shower, actually. Both of us. Celebrating the physical side of our marriage.

WES: That's not the point, honey. We have to go.

TONY: No, wait! Why can't you come to my party?

WILMA: It's a family obligation, Tony. Our daughter Debbie is giving a dance recital, and we feel we should be there.

TONY: Isn't that rather sudden?

WILMA: It is, Tony. But Debbie dances very much on impulse.

WES: And after Debbie dances, I have a political obligation.

TONY: Another one of those meetings on Israel?

WES: I like to think, Tony, that it's a meeting on the welfare of the entire free world.

TONY: Hey. *(With a side-glance at* LOIS*)* This is somewhat disappointing, friends.

WES: It's a question of priorities, Tony.

WILMA: Maybe we'll drop by for dessert. *(They are almost out the door.)*

TONY: Wait! *(They stop.)* Wilma: I don't believe Debbie is dancing tonight. And I'll tell you why. Because tonight is the night she attends that top-secret weight-loss clinic in the cellar of the Congregational Church.

SALLY: That's true, Wilma. You told us that just yesterday.

WILMA: She could do her dancing there!

TONY: No, she couldn't, Wilma. It would disturb the class. And as for you, Wes, I don't think you have a meeting on Israel. This is Saturday night, after all, and there's a specific injunction in Leviticus which says, "Speak not of Zion on nights when the gentiles give parties."

WES: Is that true?

SALLY: He taught the Bible, Wes.

LOIS: It's a wonderful book.

TONY: Wes, Wilma, you obviously made up these inept excuses on the way over. There must be a far more profound reason why you feel you can't come. *(They look at each other.)*

WES: *(Finally)* There is, Tony.

WILMA: There really is.

TONY: Then out with it, friends.

WILMA: Well . . . (SHE *sits on the couch.)*

WES: It's too much for us, buddy. This perfect party. (HE *sits beside her.)*

WILMA: The pressure . . .

WES: The sense of being so totally on the line . . .

WILMA: And now to be *judged* . . .

WES: By a New *Yorker* . . . (HE *holds his head.)*

WILMA: Oh, Tony, it's tough enough going to any party these days, let alone a perfect one.

WES: So we thought we'd go to the movies instead.

SALLY: It's interesting how people keep turning toward the movies.

LOIS: They are looking like a rather attractive alternative.

WILMA: At least you don't have to make so much *effort* at the movies.

WES: Except with Meryl Streep.

WILMA: You can never tell what accent she's doing.

SALLY: If she ruins one more book for me. . . .

WES: Is she in *The Color Purple*?

TONY: Now *wait!* Hold on! Wes! Wilma! What is this? You guys are supposed to be the mainstay of the evening.

WES: Maybe that's the trouble, Tony. Maybe you're putting too much on us.

WILMA: That's exactly it. You expect too much of your friends, Tony. I've sensed it for some time. Last week, when we were playing bridge, I heard this great groan of disappointment every time I lost a trick.

WES: And she wasn't even your partner.

WILMA: Or when we eat out together, and I order the chicken, I'm aware of your eyes on me, Tony. You make me think I should have ordered the veal.

SALLY: This has the ring of truth.

WES: We're just simple suburban people, Tony. All right, maybe I'm a urologist with a prestigious appointment at a major medical school . . .

WILMA: And maybe I'm a speech therapist in the local school system, with a strong side interest in ceramics . . .

WES: But still, we're just an ordinary middle-class couple, Tony. And glad to be so.

TONY: No, goddamnit! I don't accept that! You guys are easily capable of giving the suburbs a good name!

WES: Oh, hey . . .

TONY: I'm serious. In some ways, you stand for the full flowering of the American dream.

WILMA: Oh now . . .

TONY: *(Sitting on the arm of the couch)* You do! Your rich ethnic roots, your pleasant home throbbing with the hum of working appliances, your weedless lawn with its well-placed shrubs, your over-educated children—well hell, you folks embody the best of that particular lifestyle, that's all.

WES: Go easy.

TONY: How can I go easy when I feel so strongly on the subject. Support me on this one, Sally.

SALLY: It's true, Wes and Wilma. He may sound fatuous, but he really admires you both.

LOIS: Yes, but do they belong at this party? They feel they don't, and I tend to agree with them.

TONY: No, no. They're fine people. You wait: They'll rise to the occasion as they always have. Won't you, Wes? Wilma?

WILMA: I'm not sure we can, Tony. We're too nervous.

WES: Tell him what we did this afternoon, we were so nervous.

WILMA: We want to our family therapist this afternoon.

WES: With the kids . . .

WILMA: Except for Debbie.

WES: And we shared with him our concerns about this party.

WILMA: And you know what he said, Tony? He said that our anxiety was based on the fact that, deep down, Wes and I are desperate to be a big hit.

WES: That's what he said. He said that Wilma and I have secret fantasies of being the life of this party.

WILMA: And the kids agreed!

TONY: But then here's your chance, guys! Make your move!

WILMA: No, Tony, no. The spotlight's too much on us.

WES: You don't throw a couple of amateurs onto the center court of Wimbledon, Tony.

WILMA: Our very eagerness to succeed has incapacitated us.

TONY: Then rise above it, folks. You've done it before. What about the DeVitas' Christmas party? That was straight hardball, and you came through then.

WES: That's true. We did. *(To* WILMA*)* Particularly you, honey.

WILMA: Oh stop.

TONY: No, it's true. You guys were spectacular at the DeVitas'. I watched you working the crowd.

WILMA: Will the DeVitas be here? That might help. (*To* LOIS) I always do well around the DeVitas.

TONY: No, the DeVitas will not be here, Wilma, and I'll tell you why. Rose DeVita loses concentration on every subject she touches. She becomes difficult to follow, and when she's been drinking, well nigh impossible.

SALLY: Tony thought of inviting Monty DeVita without her.

TONY: Yes I did. I seriously thought of that. Because Monty can focus. The trouble is, lately he focuses too much. He seems to be only interested in the Dallas Cowboys, and who cares about them?

WES: I do.

TONY: Well I don't, Wes. So the DeVitas are out. *(Pause; with regret)* Betty and Dick Washburn are out, too.

WILMA: I know. They called me. They're very upset.

TONY: I can't help that. Betty Washburn talks about nothing but Dick, and Dick doesn't talk at all. I told Betty on the phone—I called her specially—and said, "Broaden your range, Betty. Or at least broaden Dick." She said she'd try.

WILMA: Still, it's so cruel, cutting people out that way.

TONY: Well if it will make you feel any better, Wilma, I told both the Washburns and the DeVitas they could come to the party if they just stayed in the bedroom and watched TV and didn't try to participate in any of the dialogue.

SALLY: It's true. He did that.

TONY: But they all thought it over and decided to stay home.

WILMA: Everything you say just makes me feel the pressure all the more.

WES: She's sensitive on these things, Tony. So am I.

TONY: Which is another good reason why I want you guys here! You bring with you a sensitivity which comes from five thousand years of Jewish anxiety. *(A stunned moment)*

WILMA: Jewish? You invited us because we were Jewish?

WES: I have a problem with that, Tony.

LOIS: So do I!

SALLY: Yes, Tony! Honestly!
(They all begin to protest noisily.)

TONY: *(Shouting them down)* All I meant was . . . *(They quiet down.)* All I meant was that Wes and Wilma are like the cellos in a Verdi ensemble. They provide a lovely, consistent, melancholy sound under the lighter, more eccentric melodies sung by some of our superficial guests. *(To WES and WILMA)* The very fact that you came over here just now, in obvious disarray, to express your concern, says something about your Jewish sense of social responsibility.
(The protesting begins again. All talk simultaneously.)

SALLY: Worse and worse.

WES: Now, I'm feeling vaguely stereotyped.

WILMA: Yes, I'm still having trouble with that, Tony.

LOIS: I'm particularly sensitive, coming as I do from New York . . .

TONY: *(Shouting them down)* All right, all right! Skip it! But can I count on you two tonight? Will you both go home, and change into what I'm sure are particularly fashionable clothes, since you must obviously have relatives in the garment industry. *(The loudest protests yet)*

Sorry! Really! I'm flailing around here simply because I don't want my cello section to walk out on me right before the opera begins! Now what say, folks? Are you with me or not?

WES: Excuse me, Tony. This calls for consultation.
*(*WES *takes* WILMA U. *to consult.* TONY, SALLY *and* LOIS *watch them.)*

TONY: *(To* LOIS*)* If they leave, I'm lost.

LOIS: I'm afraid that's true. The Jewish middle class is primarily responsible for keeping culture alive in this country.

TONY: I agree. *(Finally)*

WES: *(Coming* D. *with* WILMA*)* All right, Tony. We'll make a deal with you, because we're old and good friends.

TONY: Name your terms, Wes and Wilma.

WES: We'll come to the party if we don't feel we have to be perfect all the time.

WILMA: That's right, Tony. We want to be able to dare to fail.

WES: Our grandparents didn't come to this country from the shtetls of eastern Europe in order to feel pressured at a party, Tony. Now there it is. Take it or leave it.

TONY: I'll take it, of course!

WILMA: Oh good!

SALLY: Thank God.
(They all embrace.)

TONY: And I'll even up you one! Once the party gets going, you both should feel free to explore your own Jewishness even in front of our shallowest Protestant friends.

WES: That's great, Tony! I've always wanted to do that!

SALLY: It's getting close to that time, folks.

WILMA: Let's cut through by the Millworth's hot tub. *(They start out.)*

TONY: Oh, but wait . . .

SALLY: *(Frustratedly)* Let them get *dressed*, Tony!

TONY: I just have two quick points to add to our deal.

WES: Uh oh.

TONY: No, seriously. Wilma: when you get going out there, when the party is in full swing, try not to talk about your children.

WILMA: I love my children!

TONY: I know you do, Wilma, and so do I. But people who don't have any find it difficult to contribute to the conversation. And those who do, immediately want to talk about their own.

WILMA: I *hate* it when they do that. It's so boring.

TONY: Then don't give them the chance, Wilma. And, Wes . . .

WES: *(Suspiciously)* Here it comes.

TONY: I have to ask you not to bring up Israel.

WES: *What?*

TONY: I'm asking you that as a favor, Wes.

WES: I feel strongly about Israel.

TONY: I know you do, Wes, and I'm impressed by your commitment. But I'm asking you not to talk about it tonight.

WES: You didn't invite any Palestinians, did you?

TONY: Yes I did, Wes! *(General uproar, once again)* But they sent their regrets. Along with a very nice wedge of goat's milk cheese.

WES: O.K., I'll avoid Israel.

TONY: Good. Now get going. Both of you.

WILMA: Can we grab a shrimp or two on the way out?

TONY: You can, if you brush your teeth afterwards. Now so long.

SALLY: *(Joining them)* I'll see you to the door. And then continue to fuss reluctantly with food and flowers.
(SALLY, WES, *and* WILMA *go out. Pause.)*

TONY: *(To* LOIS*)* That handles that.

LOIS: Yes . . .

TONY: *(Raising his glass)* And the ship sails on.

LOIS: Yes.

TONY: I must say you stayed strangely in the background during that little confrontation, Lois.

LOIS: Did I?

TONY: I mean, you participated. But only occasionally. And your lines didn't have much energy or bite.

LOIS: *My* lines are not at issue here, Tony. I'm more concerned about yours.

TONY: Is something bothering you?

LOIS: Yes, Tony. There is.

TONY: Then let me have it. Now. We've only got a few minutes before the party begins, and I want to absorb it, integrate it, and act on it, if I can, before I greet my guests.

LOIS: Tony . . . *(Pause)* Tony, I think I've already said how much I admire what you're trying to do here. A perfect party. There's something big about that, and, as we've said, something quintessentially American. Only in these United States could such a notion arise. It smacks of Whitman, and Gatsby, and Citizen Kane.

TONY: Thank you, Lois.

LOIS: No, I mean it. There's something huge and grandiose about it, yes, and tragic, too. To think that one man, in his own home, would try to crystallize the hopes and dreams of an entire nation . . .

TONY: *(Looking at her suspiciously)* Somewhere in your thick syntax, Lois, I'm beginning to sense a "but," waiting to pounce . . .
(HE *passes her the hors d'oeuvres.)*

LOIS: But . . . *But*, Tony. (SHE *takes an hor d'oeuvre.)* Mmmm, this is good. But . . . Tony, I'm going to have to pass on this party.

TONY: Pass?

LOIS: It's an expression we use in New York. It means default. Withdraw. Walk.

TONY: Walk?

LOIS: After I finish my wine, Tony, and possibly one more of those delicious hors d'oeuvres . . . (TONY *passes her the tray.* SHE *takes it, holds it on her lap, and eats as she talks.)* . . . Thank you, my friend . . . I'm going to get up and walk out that door and not come back.

TONY: Now wait a minute.

LOIS: *(During mouthfuls of hors d'oeuvres)* I don't intend to write up this party, Tony. I don't intend to mention it in a casual column, nor will I refer to it in subsequent reportage. I've had a pleasant half hour or so conferring with you and your lovely wife, and meeting your suburban friends, but I'm afraid that's as far as it goes.

TONY: But you decided to review us.

LOIS: I've changed my mind.

TONY: But if you don't, that would mean that this whole evening would pass unheralded, unjudged, and uncommemorated.

LOIS: Yes.

TONY: But then the world would little note, nor long re-member, what we do here.

LOIS: That's right. Yes.

TONY: But don't you realize this is the first major cultural contribution a Protestant has made to this country since Cole Porter wrote *Kiss Me, Kate*?

LOIS: I'm sorry, Tony.

TONY: But what's happened? Why leave us now?

LOIS: Let me try to explain it, to myself as well as to you. (SHE *thinks.*) For some time now, Tony, I've had the sense that there's something vital missing here tonight.

TONY: Something vital?

LOIS: (SHE *begins to circle around the room.*) Something . . . fundamental. At first, I thought it was simply a question of language. I mean we've all been very talky around here. Very literary, and all that. And what I thought I missed was the natural vulgarity and rich rhythms of the contemporary American vernacular.

TONY: I'm not going to wander around saying "fuck" and "shit" at my own party!

LOIS: Of course you're not, Tony, and I don't blame you. It's not our stilted language that's getting me down. The source of my unhappiness lies elsewhere. *(Pause)* Now how do I put this? (SHE *sees the light.*) There's no sense of danger at this party.

TONY: Danger?

LOIS: Danger. Every good party has, underneath it, a fun-damental sense of danger. And this party has none.

TONY: But I'll have to go back to teaching if it doesn't work.

LOIS: That's frightening, Tony, but it's not frightening enough. If you want this party reviewed, then it's got to be much scarier. Think, for example, of the great parties of history: the revels of Nero during the burning of Rome. The soirées at Versailles under the lengthening shadow of the guillotine. The last frantic dance on the deck of the Titanic. Those were dangerous parties, and I'm afraid this can't equal them.

TONY: You're asking for too much, Lois.

LOIS: Maybe I am, but so are you. Oh look, my friend, we're very much alike, you and I. We are born perfectionists. I have struggled out of the polyglot mire of a Brooklyn kindergarten toward the cool, clear vision of some social ideal. You, on the other hand, carry with you the memory of a civilized past gleaned from your corrupt and decadent ancestors. I am moving up. You are moving down. We have gravitated toward one another all our lives, like two lost planets in search of a sun. There's a tremendous magnetism between us, and if you weren't happily married, I think I'd initiate an affair with you immediately. But there's no danger here, Tony. None. Even a simple birthday party is infused with the sadness of passing time. A wedding is fraught with the perils of sex. A funeral throbs with the ache of last things. Behind the best human gathering is a sense of its own precariousness. We should dance on the edge of the abyss. And that's what I don't sense here, Tony. What is the threat? Where is the pain? It's all cozy and comfortable and polite. In fact, it's so polite, Tony, that you've let me make much too long a speech without interrupting me. It's symptomatic of the whole problem.

TONY: I'll interrupt you now!

LOIS: Yes, but you don't like doing it. You're a nice man with a pretty wife, and from all reports, several fine children. You were born with money, and you married more of it, and you've lived easily all your life. The gods have been good to you, Tony, and it shows. There's an aura of smug self-congratulation which pervades this house, coupled with the insidious influence of Oscar Wilde. But there's no danger here, so it isn't a perfect party, and I feel no need to review it. (SHE *holds out her hand.*) Thank you at least for a pleasant preliminary. I hope things go reasonably well, and everyone has a perfectly adequate time. (SHE *slaps him patronizingly on the back and starts for the door.*)

TONY: Wait! I could add danger.

LOIS: *(At the door)* How?

TONY: Well I mean I could invite someone else at the last minute. Some Neo-Nazi. Some escaped convict.

LOIS: No, Tony . . .

TONY: I could have a small nuclear device ticking away in the cellar . . .

LOIS: Tony, please.

TONY: Why *not*?

LOIS: It would seem dragged in, and I'd have to say as much, when I reviewed it. (SHE *is almost out the door.*)

TONY: No, wait! Please! Really! (HE *thinks quickly.*) What about my brother?
(LOIS *stops and turns.*)

LOIS: Your brother?

TONY: My twin brother. I've invited him.

LOIS: What's his name?

TONY: Tod.

LOIS: Tod?

TONY: Tod. Though his nickname is Toad.

LOIS: Either way, that's German for . . .

TONY: Death.
(LOIS *comes back into the room.*)

LOIS: Is he . . . dangerous?

TONY: He's a killer.

LOIS: A murderer?

TONY: No. But he kills things.

LOIS: Cats? Hamsters? Things of that ilk?

TONY: No, he kills something else. He kills moments. He destroys moods. He annihilates atmospheres. *(LOIS sits on the arm of the couch.)*

LOIS: Tell me more.

TONY: I'll try. I'm the older, by half an hour. According to my mother, I was a perfect baby, and slid smilingly into the world. She was in the recovery room, celebrating my birthday with my father—raising a glass of champagne, sending a telegram to Yale, all that—when suddenly she gave a shriek and spilled her champagne. Out came Tod, who kicked and screamed and totally ruined the party.

LOIS: Your poor mother.

TONY: I know. It was as if, even then, even at his birth, Tod was a kind of afterthought, a kind of instinctive counter-argument or contradiction, emerging from the same source.

LOIS: Do you look alike, you and Tod?

TONY: Almost exactly. He, of course, wears a mustache, while I, as you may have noticed, don't. After his birth, he struggled so much against his mother's embrace that she inadvertently dropped him. The infant broke his right leg, which was improperly reset, because he irritated the doctor. The result is that he has a pronounced limp, which gives him a certain Byronic appeal, but makes him a consistently disappointing tennis partner.

LOIS: How sad.

TONY: Yes. He was such an unhappy child that my mother sent him to sunny Italy for junior high school. He returned with a book on the Borgias and the permanent speech patterns of a Neapolitan pickpocket.

LOIS: Any other distinguishing characteristics?

TONY: Just one.

LOIS: And what is that?

TONY: He has—*(HE stops.)* Never mind. It's not important. The point is that my brother is, or can be, an ultimately destructive human being. He is in constant competition with me, and everyone else. He has hacked his way through life's dark wood leaving a long, bloody spoor of victims behind him. He has been married at least four times, and divorced only twice. He was expelled from the Teamsters Union, and reprimanded by the C.I.A. His conversation is designed to make you thoroughly uncomfortable and even while he's doing it, you feel he's glancing over your shoulder, seeking out someone else to irritate even more. In short, he is probably the most dangerous person I have ever known, and already I'm having strong second thoughts about inviting him to this party.

LOIS: You said there was another characteristic which distinguished Tod from you.

TONY: Oh well. It's not important really.

LOIS: Tell me. It might prove to be helpful, later on.

TONY: I thought you were leaving.

LOIS: Frankly, now I'm on the fence. The notion of twins has always had a primitive appeal. It might just work at a party. I'm also intrigued by the mustache and the limp, and the Italian connection is unsettling. So tell me: what else does he have that you don't?

TONY: Well, to put it frankly, Lois, he has a considerably larger penis. *(Long pause)*

LOIS: I've decided to stay at this party.

TONY: You have?

LOIS: Yes. I've decided that the party may have some potential.

TONY: I'm delighted! I hope you won't be disappointed.

LOIS: That remains to be seen. *(The sound of a party begins to be heard offstage.)*

TONY: People are beginning to arrive. I should go greet my guests.

LOIS: *(Taking his arm)* I'll join you. To look them over. And to see if your brother Tod is among them.

TONY: He might not come.

LOIS: Why not?

TONY: Simply because I invited him.

LOIS: What if you called him and told him to stay away?

TONY: Then he'd show up immediately.

LOIS: Go make that call. I'm eager to meet this man. (SHE *goes out.* HE *follows, after looking back into the room with an expression of both relief and dismay.)*

END OF ACT I

ACT II

AT RISE: *The study is empty. The door to the hall is open. Sounds of the party waft in. It doesn't seem to be going very well. Then* WES *and* WILMA *enter. They are now dressed for the party:* WES *wears a tuxedo,* WILMA *a long dress.*

WES: What do you think you're doing out there?

WILMA: Me?

WES: Just what do you think you're doing?

WILMA: I am carrying on a series of decent conversations.

WES: Bullshit!

WILMA: I am keeping the party afloat!

WES: Double bullshit!

WILMA: I am partying like mad!

WES: That's not partying you're doing out there! That's crap! That's bullshit! You are shitting all over the floor out there! (HE *goes to shut the door.*)

WILMA: Where? Name a time!

WES: When you were talking with that man by the bar.

WILMA: I was good with that man.

WES: You were lousy with that man, Wilma! You were totally irresponsible!

WILMA: He was telling me about his dog.

WES: And what did you tell him?

WILMA: I told him about our cat.

WES: Jesus, Wilma.

WILMA: Well, I had to say something.

WES: What we do with our cat is a private matter!

WILMA: Well I couldn't talk about our children.

WES: And then you shifted the subject to urban renewal.

WILMA: What's wrong with that?

WES: It was a lousy transition, Wilma, and you know it. It was fake, and false, and you could hear the gears grinding all over the room!

WILMA: Well I got bored with animals.

WES: That's not the point. You don't just suddenly slam a conversation into reverse! Jesus! It was pathetic. The poor guy practically dropped his drink.
(HE *gets a cube of ice from the bar, puts it in a towel, and holds it to his head.*)

WILMA: Well I don't see you lighting any fires out there tonight.

WES: I'm doing O.K.

WILMA: You are walking through it.

WES: I'm doing fine.

WILMA: You are a zombie. You are phoning it in. I saw you slouching on the couch with that man from Rhode Island.

WES: What's wrong with him?

WILMA: Nothing, except that he ravaged his own cleaning woman.

WES: He didn't ravage her, Wilma.

WILMA: He most certainly did. She's out there right now, by the vegetable dip, confirming the incident.

WES: Well he and I didn't discuss that.

WILMA: I'll bet you didn't.

WES: We didn't. I was advising him on his hernia.

WILMA: Bore me some more, Wes.

WES: Better me on the hernia, than you on the cat!

WILMA: Listen, I may have been crude out there. I may have forced a transition or two. But at least I was reaching out towards other people and other subjects. I didn't retreat, and commandeer the couch, and indulge in a lot of macho chest-thumping and groin-scratching with a ruptured rapist from Rhode Island!
(WES *grabs her and begins to twist her arm.* SALLY *enters hurriedly, closing the door behind her.*)

SALLY: You're fighting, aren't you?
(WES *and* WILMA *separate quickly.*)

WILMA: Oh no, not really.

WES: We were just kind of sparring around, Sally.

SALLY: Oh, God, this party. It doesn't seem to be gelling at all. Everywhere I go, middle-class married couples are bickering irritably over trivial issues. Our younger friends have gone upstairs slamming the doors to the guest room, where they smoke dope and listen to loud, shrieking songs, with lyrics which are virtually incomprehensible. To avoid the din, the older folks have congealed in a gloomy corner, where they reminisce about Lawrence Welk and accuse each other of having Alzheimer's disease. Our Black and Hispanic friends, once so full of life, are huddled in sullen groups, discussing social inequities in a vaguely revolutionary tone. The gays and born-agains eye the goings-on with some contempt, depressed with our condition and their own. Even the caterers are losing interest. The bartender plies his trade with cynical abandon, confusing gin with vodka, spilling the bourbon, and stinting on the ice. The miserable maids prowl around the room, offering stale hors d'oeuvres and then snatching them away, before you've even had a chance to grab one. From off in the kitchen come sounds of an angry clatter, and unnecessary breakage, which, I am sure, we will be overcharged for later. *(By now,* SHE *has collapsed on the couch in despair.)*

WES: It sounds like an image of America itself.

SALLY: Whatever it is, it is hardly a party, much less a perfect one. And to make things worse, I can't find Tony anywhere. I'm terrified he's doing something desperate.

WILMA: I think I saw him going into the bathroom.

WES: You're not supposed to notice things like that at a party.

WILMA: *(Furiously to* WES*) Well I did*! *(Then to* SALLY*)* I also noticed that he had with him a small tin of black shoe polish.

SALLY: Black shoe polish? Then he *is* desperate. Tony hates to shine his shoes, particularly at a party.

WILMA: I wish Wes here would shine his occasionally.

WES: *(Threateningly)* I don't know about my shoes, Wilma, but I know something of yours that needs a little blacking!

SALLY: Wes! Wilma! Please! You see what's happening? Now you're talking about wife abuse, which I've always felt was basically counterproductive.

WES: You're right, Sally. I apologize. For both of us.

WILMA: *(Indignantly)* I can goddam well apologize for myself!

SALLY: Now stop! We promised Tony we'd help make the evening a success, and here we are contributing to the disaster. Look at us, arguing in here, while that strange critic pokes around from room to room, like a dental hygienist in a ceaseless search for cavities. Oh I give up. I really do. The hell with it all. It just confirms what I've told Tony all along: there's no possibility for a civilized social life in America beyond the comforts of a few friends and the ghastly confines of the family.

WES: *(Joining her on the couch)* Come on, Sally. We can do better.

WILMA: *(Sitting on her other side)* Yes, Sally. Please. Let's try again.

WES: Don't be discouraged, Sally. Listen. Most parties hit a snag during the course of the evening. We learned about it in medical school. It's called hitting the wall. Or going into the tunnel. It happens even in Europe. The best thing we can do is drink plenty of liquids and ride out the pain.

SALLY: I wish I could believe that, Wes.

WILMA: No, it's good reliable advice, Sally. But perhaps I can add something, gleaned from my experience as a semi-professional potter. Let me say that a party is like a pot in process. It can't be pushed or prodded or poked. *(SALLY blinks.)*

WES: You're spitting a little, Wilma.

WILMA: That's because I feel *passionate* on the subject. *(WES hands SALLY a handkerchief. SALLY wipes her face.)* What we've got to do now, Sally, is nurse this party. Caress it. Stroke it into shape. These are particularly feminine virtues, Wes, but you're welcome to watch.

SALLY: But what about Tony? This whole damn thing was his idea, and why should we bother, if he isn't even there?

WES: Maybe he is, and you just haven't seen him, Sally. It's a poor party indeed when husbands and wives hover around each other. For example, I plan to ditch Wilma as soon as I leave this room.

WILMA: It's true, Sally. He will. And I accept that. Men are like children at parties. They like to wander off, but they always scamper back for reassurance at the breast.

SALLY: *(Getting to her feet with a sigh)* I'll try to believe that. Come on. Let's give it another go.

WES: Do you think we should all do a few stretch exercises first?

SALLY: *(Going to the door)* No, no. Come on. There are times when you've simply got to go on faith in human nature.
(SHE *opens the door.* LOIS, *who has been eavesdropping, tumbles in.)* Oh hi, Lois.

WILMA: Hi, Lois.

WES: Hi, Lois.

SALLY: Did you hear what we were saying, Lois?

LOIS: Of course not. Did you say anything important?

SALLY: Yes, actually. We were all just saying what a wonderful party this is.

WES: That's right. We were all just congratulating ourselves on how well things were going.

LOIS: Well none of that came through. I *did* happen to hear, however, someone compare a critic to a dental hygienist.

SALLY: Oh dear.

LOIS: I'd be careful of cracks like that, people. There will always be critics, and you're lucky enough to get a good one.

SALLY: Well all I know is I'm having a wonderful time!

WILMA: So am I. Aren't you Lois? Aren't you having fun?

LOIS: I never comment till it's over. A responsible judge should always weigh all the evidence, good and bad, before imposing the death sentence.

SALLY: Oh dear. Maybe we'd better join the party. Come, come, dear friends. Let's enjoy ourselves even more before the party ends.

(SALLY *herds* WES *and* WILMA *out as the party sounds come up.* LOIS *remains onstage.* SHE *takes a compact out of her purse, and begins to comb her hair, using the mirror to glance behind her. After a moment,* TOD *comes in. He wears a tuxedo, and looks just like* TONY, *except that he has a black mustache, slicked-back hair, and a pronounced limp.* LOIS *watches him in the mirror as he closes the study door behind him. The party sounds die out.)*

TOD: *(Speaking throughout in a corny Italian accent.)* You Lois?

LOIS: I try to be, at least during daylight hours.

TOD: How about at night?

LOIS: Oh well, then I'm the Queen of Rumania.
(TOD *comes farther into the room; he drags his foot behind him in an exaggerated limp. He might sing Italian words seductively, "Spaghetti" . . . "Spumoni" . . . "Scongili" . . . etc. Finally:)*

TOD: Would you like to see my cock?

LOIS: I beg your pardon?

TOD: I said I've been drinking since seven o'clock.

LOIS: I hope you're still in control of all your faculties.

TOD: Goddam right, you stupid mother.

LOIS: What?

TOD: I said I thought I might have another. (HE *limps to the bar.)* May I mix you one?

LOIS: I don't think so, thank you.

TOD: It would do you good, you silly snatch.

LOIS: Excuse me?

TOD: I can easily mix you up a special batch.

LOIS: No thank you. No. Thank you.

TOD: *(Beginning to circle around her)* Tell me about yourself, Lois.

LOIS: Where do I begin?

TOD: Do you like to fuck?

LOIS: Only when I laugh.

TOD: You're making it hard for me.

LOIS: Don't hold it against me.

TOD: You're turning me on. I have a weakness for repressed women.

LOIS: What makes you think I'm repressed?

TOD: I can tell. You're all bottled up.

LOIS: You think so?

TOD: Oh yes. Luckily, I like to open bottles. Particularly with my teeth.

LOIS: You're wasting your time.

TOD: Am I?

LOIS: Oh yes. I'm much more at home with the twist-off top.
(TOD sits down beside her on the couch.)

TOD: You've got all the right answers, don't you, Lois?

LOIS: That's because I'm on to you. I know all about you.

TOD: What do you know? Be specific. Be concrete. *(HE adjusts his stiff leg.)*

LOIS: I know, for example, that you've been out there wandering around from person to person, group to group, sowing seeds of dissension. I know you're here to systematically destroy your own brother's party.

TOD: Well, you're wrong on that, Lois. I'm here to salvage it.

LOIS: Ha, ha. That's a good one. Ha, ha, ha. How, pray tell?

TOD: By giving you such a fucking good time in bed, Lois, that you'll stagger bowlegged back to your word processor and write an out-and-out rave!

LOIS: Ha, ha. And how do you propose to get me into that bed, Tod?

TOD: Well first, of course, I plan to give you a good, stiff drink.
(HE *gets up and goes to the bar again.*)

LOIS: I don't want a drink, Tod. I believe I've already indicated as much.

TOD: You'll want one, Lois, after you see what I'm making.
(HE *begins mixing a concoction in a silver cocktail shaker.*)

LOIS: Does it have a local habitation and a name?

TOD: I call it a Cardinal Sin.

LOIS: Then I won't like it. I have strong reservations about the Catholic hierarchy, coming as I do from New York.

TOD: I think you'll love this one, Lois. I think you'll lap it up.
(HE *works on the drink.*)

LOIS: Suppose I take a sip of this drink. Suppose I even chug-a-lug it. What happens next?

TOD: Well, of course, by then I'd be sitting beside you. And what I'd do is put my arm around you, and slowly caress your left breast until your nipple was firm and erect.

LOIS: But I wouldn't allow that, Tod. I'd take your hand and remove it with my own.

TOD: You wouldn't be able to, Lois. Both your hands would be thoroughly preoccupied.

LOIS: Preoccupied?

TOD: Yes. One would be holding the Cardinal Sin.

LOIS: All right. I'll grant that. But the other?

TOD: The other would be perched, like a frightened bird, on my throbbing loins.

LOIS: Hmmm.

TOD: You see. You get the picture? *(HE continues to concoct the drink.)*

LOIS: I'm afraid I don't, Tod. I mean here we are in the middle of a party. People are bursting through that door every other minute.

TOD: That's why I'd maneuver you immediately to the master bedroom, under the pretext of showing you pictures of children and dogs.

LOIS: But still, people would come in and out. Visiting the bathroom. Combing their hair. Getting their coats, if the party continues to degenerate.

TOD: We'd solve that problem with Vaseline.

LOIS: Vaseline? Don't be foolish. Vaseline solves many problems, but not that one.

TOD: We'll put it on the doorknob, Lois, rendering it virtually unturnable.
(HE moves toward her again.)

LOIS: You have an answer for everything, don't you?

TOD: I believe I do. Yes.

LOIS: Well I'm still not sure I'd like such a situation, with people banging on the door and rattling the doorknob. I think I'd be distracted.

TOD: *(Sitting behind her, on the back of the couch)* You wouldn't hear a thing, Lois. And I'll tell you why. Because by that time you would be writhing naked on the bed, among the furs and Burberrys, emitting a series of wild exuberant love cries, ending in a veritable Vesuvian eruption of delight. People will be running for cover, Lois. You'll be scattering red hot lava over a relatively large area. And then, while you're still smoldering, maybe smoking occasionally but temporarily inactive, I'm going to take you into the bathroom, and give you a bath, and anoint your erogenous zones with Oil of Olay. And then dial your editor in New York, and hand you the telephone, and you're going to say into that phone, "Truly this was a perfect party, and I'm mighty glad I came." *(Pause)*

LOIS: You think I can be bought, don't you?

TOD: Yes I do.

LOIS: Know what I think, Tod?

TOD: No. What do you think, Lois?

LOIS: I think you've said those things hoping I'll be shocked. I think you want me to reject that drink, repulse your advances, and run from this room. I think you want me to pan this poor party in no uncertain terms.

TOD: You think that?

LOIS: Yes I do. But it won't happen, Tod. Bring me that drink immediately.
(HE hobbles back to the bar to get the drink. He might sing a few more Italian words as he goes. He brings the drink, it is a weird, bubbling, bright red potion, emitting smoke. SHE takes it, looks at it and smiles.) A Cardinal Sin, eh?

TOD: That's what it's called in *The Story of O*, Lois.

LOIS: Down the hatch, with a one-two-three. *(SHE slugs it down, then slams the glass on the coffee table.)* There. I intend to take you on and top you, Tod, point by point, game by game. The bets aren't in yet, and the match isn't over. *(SHE stands up.)* So show me that master bedroom. Let's strip for action, and commence firing.

And when everything's said and done, I want you to
know that I still intend to assess this evening with a
clear, unjaundiced eye!
(HE *grabs her and kisses her. Immediately,* SALLY *opens the
door and comes in.*)

SALLY: Ah, Tony! Here you are!
(TOD *breaks away from the kiss and looks at her.*)
   Oh. Excuse me. I thought you were my husband, Tony.

TOD: No. I'm Tod. His twin brother.

SALLY: I see. I'm terribly sorry.
(SHE *goes out.*)

TOD: *(To* LOIS) Goddammit, but you're a tough nut to
crack, Lois.

LOIS: If there are any nuts to be cracked around here, Tod,
let them be yours.

(SHE *goes out grimly.* TONY *looks after her nervously,
finishes the rest of the Cardinal Sin from the cocktail
shaker. Then he starts off after her, remembers to limp,
and almost catches his leg in the door as he leaves. A
moment. Then* WES *leads* WILMA *into the room. He
closes the door behind him, looks at her, and then kisses
her.*)

WILMA: What was that for?

WES: You know.

WILMA: I'm afraid I don't.

WES: You were fantastic out there!

WILMA: Really?

WES: You were terrific.

WILMA: Well thanks.

WES: You turned the whole thing around.

WILMA Well I made an effort. I'll say that.

WES: Effort? You were flying out there! You went into orbit out there! What got into you?

WILMA: I don't know, Wes. The vibrations changed, or something. I just got on a roll.

WES: Roll? You were spinning! No one got *near* you.

WILMA: *You* got near me, Wes.

WES: Oh, well . . .

WILMA: No, I'm serious. When that woman fell asleep in the corner? Who helped me slap her awake and get her going?

WES: Yeah well . . .

WILMA: I mean it. And when that older man tried to sneak out and go home, who threw a body-block on him in the front hall?

WES: Well, it was fun. I'll say that.

WILMA: *(Hugging him)* What a party! I can't wait to take this experience home and share it with our children.

WES: Sshh!
(They break apart and look toward the door.)

WILMA: *(Whispering)* If we present it right, if we don't intrude on their private space or personal time, I think they might enjoy hearing about it.

WES: Yes, but I've got another idea.

WILMA: What?

WES: I want to sneak home and get our cat.

WILMA: Get our cat?

WES: Get it. Bring it here. And display it.

WILMA: Dis*play* it?

WES: To the group at large.

WILMA: You love that cat, don't you, Wes?

WES: Yes, I do.

WILMA: You're extremely attached to that animal.

WES: Yes, I am. Shall I get it?

WILMA: *(Holding him; gently)* I'm going to say no on that, Wes. And I'll tell you why. It might serve as a conversation piece for two or three minutes. But then people will drift away. Or the cat will.

WES: I suppose you're right.

WILMA: After all, it can't talk.

WES: Thank God.

WILMA: Exactly. *(Both laugh. The door opens.* SALLY *comes in. The party sounds come up. She closes the door quickly behind her and leans against it, breathlessly.)*

SALLY: The party's beginning to crest!

WILMA: That's just what we were saying!

SALLY: It's amazing. Everything is suddenly coming together. It's as if somewhere someone had pulled a switch, and a huge gravitational force had come into play. It's like the beginning of civilization itself, if I remember my courses at Vassar correctly. First, there was this man, I don't even remember who he was, who sat down at the piano, and started idly fiddling with the keys. Then others began to gather around. A chord was sounded. A tune emerged. Someone began to sing. And then, as if out of nowhere, people produced other musical instruments. Harps . . . xylophones . . . Moog Synthesizers . . . And now!—Well, let's listen, and see how far they've come:

(She opens the door. From offstage we hear the huge sounds of the Mormon Tabernacle Choir—full orchestra and chorus— singing the "Battle Hymn of the Republic."* A rich, romantic light and an exotic fog spill into the study as the three stagger back, amazed.)

VOICES:
. . . His Truth is marching on!

Glory, Glory Halleluia!
Glory, Glory Halleluia!
Glory, Glory Halleluia!

His Truth is marching on!

(SALLY, WES, and WILMA pick up glasses, trays, ice-buckets, as cymbals, triangles, and drums. They march around the room, ending in a wild display of sympathetic enthusiasm. Finally, SALLY closes the door and the sounds stop.)

SALLY: See?

WILMA: *(Wet-eyed, hugging her)* It's a good party, Sally.

WES: A very good party indeed.

SALLY: Or rather we should say it *was* a good party.

WES: You mean it's over?

SALLY: It will be. I doubt if we can top that. I'd better go out and say goodbye.

WILMA: Did you ever find Tony?

SALLY: No, but I imagine he was in the chorus. He's got an excellent baritone if he stays with the main melody.
(SHE opens the door and heads out into the light, closing the door behind her).

WES: Should we leave, too? Shall I get our coats?

WILMA: I imagine Tony wants us to stick around for a postmortem.

WES: That's right. What's a party without a postmortem. It should be a gas. *(Leads her to couch.)* Come on. Let's relax. *(They sit down side by side.)* There's nothing like a good party to bring you together. *(They settle back, romantically.)*

WILMA: Mmm. This is lovely.

WES: Mmm hmmm. *(HE thinks)* Out there, when we were going strong, do you think we needed a little cutting?

WILMA: Cutting?

WES: Just a snip or two. Here and there. For example, when I was talking about the function of the urethra.

WILMA: You were lovely on the urethra. You were lyrical.

WES: Still, I might tighten it up for the next party.

WILMA: Well try. See how it floats. You can always go back.

WES: Actually, you might give a little thought to that joke about your mother.

WILMA: I'm not going to change a word of that, Wes.

WES: Just think about it.

WILMA: I'm not going to lose that laugh, Wes! I'm serious!

WES: O.K., O.K.

WILMA: Honestly. You can ruin something by tinkering with it.

WES: O.K., O.K. *(The door opens.* LOIS *comes in, looking somewhat disheveled. Sounds of the party offstage indicate people are beginning to say goodbye.* LOIS *closes the door behind her.)* Oh. Hi Lois.

WILMA: Hi Lois. *(LOIS has the visible traces of black mustache on her upper lip.)*

LCIS: I'm looking for my purse.

WILMA: We thought you had left long ago.

LOIS: No. Actually, I've been . . . upstairs.

WES: Upstairs?

LOIS: Yes. The party took a strange turn in that direction, and I felt it was my duty as a critic to follow the thread. *(SHE sits down gingerly.)* Some of my colleagues, of course, have been known to leave in the middle, or rush rudely out at the end, without even saying goodbye. I don't do that, even if I have a deadline. I stick it out, to the bitter end.

(SHE powders her nose, sees the mustache, tries to figure it out, can't, powders over it.)

WES: The bitter end? I hope that doesn't reflect your opinion of the party.

LOIS: Not necessarily. The bitter end may simply mean the end of a rope, or cable, that is wound around a bitt, or post.

WILMA: Yes, but it may also mean a painful, or disastrous, conclusion.

LOIS: *(Getting up, holding out her hand)* Either way, goodnight. Nice to meet you both . . . You were interesting minor characters . . . Goodnight . . . Goodnight. *(SHE starts for the door. TONY comes in.)*

TONY: You're leaving, Lois? *(LOIS reels back with a little shriek.)* What's the matter?

LOIS: *(Regaining her composure)* I thought for a moment you were someone else.

TONY: You may have momentarily confused me with my twin brother.

LOIS: That must be it.

TONY: Then you met him?

LOIS: Oh yes. We . . . met.

WILMA: I didn't know you had a twin, Tony.

TONY: I don't broadcast it. Nobody likes to be duplicated.

LOIS: Is he still here, by the way?

TONY: No, Lois, he's gone. I saw him skulking down the back stairs, and slinking off into the night, his tail between his legs.

LOIS: Let's hope that so-called tail remains there. Frankly, Tony, I don't want to meet him again. I feel that he and I exhausted every possible topic of conversation. (SHE *holds out her hand.*) And now I must say goodbye. As you know, I have a deadline to meet.

TONY: *(Shaking hands.)* I won't ask you to say ahead of time what you'll write about us.

LOIS: No. That would be a violation of some meaningless taboo.

TONY: I'll see you to the door, though.

LOIS: That won't be necessary. I'm sure Sally is out there, giving wet, warm kisses to the last of your guests. Goodbye, Tony. *(Grimly)* And if you see that brother of yours, ask him to read my review. (SHE *goes out. Pause.)*

WES: *(Looking after her)* Something's gotten into that woman. (TONY *looks at him nervously.)*

TONY: You're right, Wes, and I'm worried.

WILMA: Why? It was a spectacular party!

TONY: You know that, I know that. But does she?

WILMA: What makes you think she doesn't?

TONY: I don't know. There's something wrong. I can feel it in my bones. (SALLY *comes in.)*

SALLY: There. That's the last of our guests.

TONY: Did Lois say anything on the way out?

SALLY: Nothing. She just put her head down and went through the line like a fullback.

TONY: Could you tell anything from her expression?

SALLY: Nothing. She seemed particularly enigmatic. Her brow was furrowed . . .

TONY: Oh God!

SALLY: But on the other hand, playing about her lips was a Mona Lisa smile.

WILMA: See, Tony? You just can't tell!

SALLY: Oh. She did say one thing, though.

EVERYONE ELSE: WHAT?

SALLY: She said that she had been invited to give a capsule edition of her review over local television at eleven twenty-seven tonight.

WES: *(Looking at his watch)* It's almost eleven twenty-seven now.

WILMA: Do you still have a TV in your study, Tony?

TONY: Actually, I do. I use it for watching *Masterpiece Theatre*.

SALLY: He uses it for watching talk shows, and wishing he could run one.

TONY: Used to, Sally. Yesterday. When I was young.

WILMA: Let's turn it *on*!
(SHE crosses to the TV cabinet, opens it, turns on TV.)

TONY: Oh God! She'll say it was terrible! She'll say the food was bad, and the drinks were worse, and the company impossible!

SALLY: Ssshh.
(They all watch the screen intently.)

TV: *(Voiceover.)* . . . And now Lois Lumkin, our guest entertainment critic from New York, will tell us where she's been and what she thought of it. *(The lights come up on LOIS's actual face, framed in the TV.)*

LOIS: *(Brightly)* Thanks, Bruce . . . Tonight's party causes me to feel emotions as mixed as its guest list. The basic idea—that someone would set out to give a perfect party—is farfetched but engaging. *(Everyone reacts enthusiastically.)* The execution is something else again. It sputters where it should sparkle, and fizzles where it should dazzle. *(Everyone looks glum.)* Perhaps I'll elaborate on these thoughts tomorrow in a major New York newspaper. Meanwhile, let me simply assign it a Seven . . .

SALLY: Seven's not bad . . .

LOIS: On a scale of Seventeen . . .

TONY: Oh Good Lord . . .

LOIS: And I had serious reservations about the lighting.

TONY: The *lighting*?

TV ANNOUNCER'S VOICE: Seen one party, seen 'em all, right, Lois? *(*LOIS *laughs charmingly.)*

SALLY: Turn that thing off.
*(*TONY *slams shut the cabinet, cutting off* LOIS *in mid-laugh. Pause.)*

TONY: Shit.

SALLY: I'm sorry, sweetie.

TONY: The lighting.

WES: What does she know, anyhow?

WILMA: Yes. What difference does it make?

TONY: *(Pacing around the room)* Difference? What difference does it make? That woman is going to sit down and write an article which will appear in New York, and here, and in Upper Volta, for Chrissake, saying that I put on a lousy show!

SALLY: Not lousy, sweetheart. Just so-so.

TONY: That broad is going to go on National Public Radio, which is beamed by satellite into the farthest reaches of the Soviet Union, and announce that she's just been to one hell of a crumby party.

SALLY: Not crumby, love. Just disappointing.

TONY: That bitch is going to hang out in various two-star New York restaurants—

SALLY: Now stop it, Tony. You're exaggerating.

WILMA: Still, isn't it a shame that one woman should have such a far-reaching effect?

SALLY: She said, "Perhaps." She might not even review it.

TONY: Worse and worse! Love me, hate me, but don't ignore me! Fuck, piss, shit! *(HE sinks into a chair. Pause.)*

WILMA: I think we'd better go. I'm uncomfortable with such explicit language, even though I recognize its therapeutic value.

WES: Actually, I get a kick out of language like that. But I'll leave too, for the sake of our marriage. *(Embraces TONY)* So long, Tony. If I could sum up the party in one word, I'd say it was interesting.

TONY: Thanks a bunch, Wes.

WILMA: *(Kissing TONY)* No really. It was. We learned several things about parties we didn't know.

WES: And several things we didn't need to know.

TONY: Get out of here, guys!

SALLY: I'll show you to the door.

WES: Don't bother, Sally. You both should have deeply personal things to say to each other at a humiliating time like this.

WILMA: Yes, but don't say them. Just go to each other, look in each other's eyes, and hold each other, tightly, for a long, long time. And let the tears come, people. Let the— *(Everyone shouts her down with groans.)*

TONY: Please *leave*, Wilma!

WES: *(At the door)* Come to think of it, Tony, the lighting *was* bad. I meant to mention it myself.

TONY: *Scram*!
(WES and WILMA go. SALLY starts to clean up. Pause. TONY looks at her.) My mother liked it. *(SALLY says nothing.)* No kidding. She said it was a lot of fun. *(Still nothing from SALLY.)* It's almost as if Lois had attended an entirely different party. Didn't she hear the singing? Jesus, what kind of a country do we live in where one person calls the critical shots? It's cultural fascism, that's what it is! It's Nazi Germany! In Moscow, they have twenty critics, and nobody pays any attention to any of them. *(Nothing.)* Well. Back to the classroom. Probably at the high school level. If I'm lucky. Teaching nothing but courses on decline and decay. Spending the rest of my days searching the puffy, narcoticized eyes of my students for some faint, dim light of recognition. Knowing all along that all they know is that I couldn't even give a decent party. *(Still nothing from SALLY as she cleans up. HE glances at her again.)* It will affect you, too, of course. I imagine you'll lose your job at the hospital once they hear about this. You'll have to retool. Take up high tech state-of-the-art software. Sell chips and bits and disks and bytes in some vast suburban shopping center, where you're the only salesperson within an area of three square miles. *(SALLY dumps the guest list into the wastebasket. He winces.)* Go on. Say it.

SALLY: Say what?

TONY: I'm a simple, shallow, smart-assed shit, and I deserved all this.

SALLY: I won't say that.

TONY: I'm a trivial-minded twit, and I had it coming.

SALLY: I won't even say that.

TONY: Then what are you going to say? Simply goodbye? Will you leave me?

SALLY: I might.

TONY: Knew it.

SALLY: It all depends on how you answer a question, Tony.

TONY: Don't tell me. Let me guess: why am I so fucking hung up on parties?

SALLY: That's not the question. My question is the oldest question in the world. It was first asked in the Bible, Genesis, Chapter Four, Verse Nine.

TONY: Wow, Sally. You've got almost total recall from Sunday School.

SALLY: My question is what God asks Cain. Namely, where is thy brother? *(Pause)*

TONY: Would you repeat the question?

SALLY: I don't think I need to, Tony. *(Pause)*

TONY: My brother, eh.

SALLY: Your brother.

TONY: Well, as I told the others, I believe he may have slinked—or slunk—anyway, I believe he has *sidled* off into the night.

SALLY: I don't believe that, Tony.

TONY: You don't believe it?

SALLY: I think he's still here.

TONY: *(Crossing to the door)* Where? In the cellar? Cultivating toadstools?

SALLY: I think he's right in this room.

TONY: My twin brother? Tod? *(Looking around the room)*

SALLY: I don't believe you have a twin brother, Tony.

TONY: But you saw him. You walked right into this room when he was kissing Lois!

SALLY: How do you know that, if you weren't there, Tony? *(Pause)*

TONY: Uh oh.

SALLY: You made up this brother, Tony, in a desperate attempt to retrieve this party. You painted a cheezy mustache, with Kiwi shoe polish, on your upper lip. You cultivated a grotesque limp and a ludicrous accent. You didn't even bother to change your costume. You simply pretended to be this so-called twin brother. *(Pause)*

TONY: How do you know I'm not my twin brother pretending to be me?

SALLY: That is a question only Pirandello could answer. Meanwhile, I'll ask another.

TONY: One is enough.

SALLY: This is simply a corollary to the first. Namely: did you or did you not copulate with that critic?

TONY: I . . .

SALLY: Yes or no.

TONY: I copulated.

SALLY: Thought so. You left your guests, you went upstairs, you put Vaseline on the doorknob, which was an old trick we used when the children were younger, and then you proceeded to have sexual relations with a woman who writes for the Arts and Leisure section of one of the finest newspapers in the entire free world.

TONY: That's all true.

SALLY: Jesus, Tony! How hungry you must have been for success!

TONY: I was. And I suppose it's no excuse to say that all Americans are.

SALLY: None at all.

TONY: I didn't think so.

SALLY: One final question.

TONY: Sally . . .

SALLY: Now this is a crucial question, and I have to put it carefully. When Lois, on television, implied that this party was disappointing, was she also referring to your sexual performance? *(Long pause)*

TONY: Yes.

SALLY: I thought so.

TONY: Are you going to leave me?

SALLY: I've got good reason to now, don't I?

TONY: Will you be taking the video cassette recorder?

SALLY: Don't jump the gun, Tony. That might have been one of your problems with Lois.

TONY: Sorry.

SALLY: You see, I'm thinking. I'm trying to put all of this together. So much has happened this evening that it takes all of my concentration just to keep these balls in the air. *(TONY winces.)* Sorry, darling. All right now, look, Tony. Let's be frank. I'm beginning to see a pattern here, and I think we should explore it before we make a final decision about our marriage.

TONY: O.K.

SALLY: Now bear with me, love. It seems to me that your attempt to achieve social perfection in the living room is echoed in your attempt to achieve sexual perfection in the bedroom.

TONY: Hmmm.

SALLY: But that's just the tip of the iceberg. This impulse to control, to shape, to achieve perception permeates the fabric of this country. For example, I think it's indicative of what's wrong with American theater.

TONY: American theater?

SALLY: And American sports. And American foreign policy, where we are attempting to impose some ideal shape on the Middle East, Central America, and Southeast Asia.

TONY: Good God, that's true.

SALLY: I think it is. In other words, you could, in a sense, say that America itself, in its middle age, is trying to give a perfect party, at home and abroad.

TONY: I never looked at things that way before.

SALLY: Well look at them that way now. Because what we're really talking about is sexual, social, cultural, and political *imperialism*, on a large and general scale!

TONY: Good Lord.

SALLY: And it doesn't *work*, Tony. It doesn't work in the bedroom, and it doesn't work outside. That's why Lois walked out of here so bitterly disappointed. And why our embassies are being attacked all over the world. And why the Yankees can't seem to win the pennant.

TONY: So in other words, all I've done tonight is take American idealism, and reveal it for the dark, destructive dream it really is.

SALLY: I'm afraid that's the long and the short of it, darling.

TONY: What a grim vision, Sally. You've opened up an abyss. It seems that a party is just a power trip.

SALLY: At least your kind of party is, my love.

TONY: Oh God it's true! So what happens now? Will you leave me?

SALLY: I've thought of that.

TONY: Go off with some angry emissary from the Third World?

SALLY I've thought of that too.

TONY: Live in a newly emerging democracy with a quasi-Marxist orientation? Experiment with alternative theater and ambivalent sexuality? Give up partnering, and parenting, and hostessing, all the days of your life?

SALLY: I've thought of all these possibilities, and rejected them out of hand.

TONY: But then where do we go from here? What happens to *us*? What happens to *me*?

SALLY: Sweetheart—

TONY: *(Getting up, coming* D.*)* No, I'm serious now. What happens to me? I know what I am now. A fifty-year-old fool, all burdened down with eighteenth-century ideals, nineteenth-century impulses, and twentieth-century despair. I've betrayed my wife, embarrassed my family, and irritated the critics! Oh I'm a hopeless case. If were Lois, I'd pan me unmercifully. What do I do with the rest of my life? My children are gone, my teaching's behind me, my wife patronizes me unbearably.

SALLY: Tony . . .

TONY: No, really. I'm totally hung up. I'm a man without illusions, which means I'm no man at all. What happens to me now?
(A door bell rings offstage.)

SALLY: There's your answer.

TONY: A door bell ringing late at night?

SALLY: That's it.

TONY: I doubt very much that it will dispell my current mood of despair. It's probably the children, all deciding to go to graduate school. Or else the I.R.S. disallowing me to deduct this party.

SALLY: Don't be cynical, Tony. It's just your friends, back for another try.

TONY: Another try?

SALLY: I told people, as they left, to take a short nap and then come back, after we'd had a chance to talk. This time, I said, it will be my party, and I'll be running it on totally different terms.

TONY: What terms?

SALLY: There will be no attempt to make this party perfect. There will be no shaping or judging or interrupting unless someone gets physically violent or is obviously misinformed. You will simply go among your friends and take them for what they are. There won't even be a caterer. Everyone is bringing over various ethnic dishes, and has promised to help clean up afterwards. *(*TONY *crosses to door, opens it, looks out. We hear the sounds of noisy chatter and rock music: "Burning Down the House" by the Talking Heads.*)*

TONY: It could turn into chaos, out there.

SALLY: That's the chance you'll have to take.

TONY: Do you mean to tell me that in that random and noisy disorder lies the future of America?

SALLY: I suppose you could say that.
*(*TONY *closes the door and returns to her.)*

TONY: I'm not sure I can live with that much ambiguity.

SALLY: You'll have to try.

TONY: But what about our personal life, Sally? Will you ever forgive me?

*See Special Note on copyright page.

SALLY: Tony: you've done some terrible things tonight. You've compromised your marriage by fornicating with a first-string reviewer. You've compromised your aesthetic sensibilities by putting foul language into the mouth of a fake twin brother. Furthermore, by inventing this brother, you went against everyone's advice and imitated Oscar Wilde. There are many wives, I'm sure, who would be thoroughly fed up. But I'm not, Tony. Through all your foolishness, I somehow sense a fundamental yearning to create a vital human community in this impossible land of ours. And so I forgive you.

TONY: Oh, thanks, Sal.
(HE *kisses her.* WES *and* WILMA *come in.* WES *has his collar open and carries a beer.* WILMA *carries a casserole covered with tinfoil.)*

WES: Come on in! The party's fine!

WILMA: And our children are here. And so are yours. And Lois has come back! *(*LOIS *comes in, carrying a large container of Kentucky Fried Chicken.)*

LOIS: Yes, and I realize that I, too, am an example of American idealism gone haywire. My standards are obviously too high. *(A lovely pink light shines on her.)* I also notice an improvement in the lighting. I plan to go back in there now and re-review everything in sight from a much more generous perspective! *(Everyone cheers. They go off dancing merrily as the music and party sounds come up loud and clear.)*

THE END

Plume

EXCITING CONTEMPORARY PLAYS

☐ **THE COLLECTED PLAYS OF NEIL SIMON, VOL 2, by Neil Simon.** From the most prolific and probably the most popular American playwright of our time come some of the best loved plays of today. Includes *Little Me; The Gingerbread Lady; The Prisoner of Second Avenue; The Sunshine Boys; The Good Doctor; God's Favorites; California Suite;* and *Chapter Two.* With a special Introduction by the author.   (263581—$14.95)

☐ **PLENTY by David Hare.** This superbly crafted, razor-edged drama takes its remarkable heroine, a former French Resistance fighter, through twenty years of postwar changes. "David Hare is the most fascinating playwright since Harold Pinter. The play is unforgettable, an enigma wrapped in mystery with repressed and smoldering sexuality and high drama."—Liz Smith, *The New York Daily News.*   (259568—$7.95)

☐ **FENCES: A Play by August Wilson.** The author of the 1984-85 Broadway season's best play, *Ma Rainey's Black Bottom*, returns with another powerful, stunning dramatic work. "Always absorbing . . . The work's protagonist—and greatest creation—is a Vesuvius of rage. . . . The play's finest moments perfectly capture that inky almost imperceptible agitated darkness just before the fences of racism, for a time, came crashing down."—Frank Rich, *The New York Times*   (264014—$7.95)

☐ **THE HOUSE OF BLUE LEAVES AND TWO OTHER PLAYS by John Guare.** Artie Shaughnessy, a zoo-keeper and aspiring songwriter, is a man with a dream— which is put on a collision course with a devastating, wildly funny reality. THE HOUSE OF BLUE LEAVES, along with two other of Guare's fierce farces, form a trio of acerbic tragicomedies that painfully and hilariously reflect our world. "Mr. Guare . . . is in a class by himself."—*The New York Times*
                    (264596—$9.95)

☐ **FOB AND OTHER PLAYS by David Henry Hwang.** From the Tony-award winning author of *M. Butterfly* comes a collection of six plays that capture the spirit, the struggles, and the secret language of the Chinese-American while exploring universal human issues. "Hwang is fast becoming the wunderkind of the American theater."—*San Francisco Chronicle*   (263239—$8.95)

Prices slightly higher in Canada.

Buy them at your local bookstore or use this convenient coupon for ordering.

NEW AMERICAN LIBRARY
P.O. Box 999, Bergenfield, New Jersey 07621

Please send me the PLUME BOOKS I have checked above. I am enclosing $_____ (please add $1.50 to this order to cover postage and handling). Send check or money order—no cash or C.O.D.'s. Prices and numbers are subject to change without notice.

Name_____

Address_____

City_____ State_____ Zip Code_____

Allow 4-6 weeks for delivery.
This offer is subject to withdrawal without notice.